Ed # 00

You're OK, Kid!®

To
Andrew & Nicholas
Stay close to Jesus
& good luck with
School.

Floyd Edward Reinhardt

You're OK, Kid!®

The Search for a Father's Love

Floyd Edward Reinhardt

Littleton Publishing Company
LITTLETON, COLORADO

First printing 2004

ISBN 0-9701567-0-7
LCCN 2003108196

ATTENTION CORPORATIONS, UNIVERSITIES, COLLEGES, AND PROFES-SIONAL ORGANIZATIONS: Quantity discounts are available on bulk purchases of this book for educational, gift purposes, or as premiums for increasing magazine subscriptions or renewals. Special books or book excerpts can also be created to fit specific needs. For information, please contact Littleton Publishing Company, 40 West Littleton Blvd., Suite 210, Littleton, CO 80120, toll free 866-876-5543; phone/ fax 303-798-1273; urokkid@aol.com; www.youreokkid.com.

You're OK, *Kid!*® is dedicated to those
whose lives have been forever changed
because of divorce

and

to those whose lives have been
changed forever
because of brain injury.

"Who will teach Eddie to smile again?" asked our daughter, Rose. "You will!" was her mother's response. And Rose did. You, Rose, have taught us to be joyful and at peace with his accident.

I want to thank my wife Patricia for her untiring work throughout the years raising our six children, guiding Eddie's recovery and loving me as we struggled to keep our marriage together.

Thanks to our sons, John, Tom, Paul and Matthew who were patient with us as we gave our time to their fallen brother. Thank you, Paul, for showing me how to turn on the computer so I could put this all in writing.

Thanks to the Eugene Register Guard for the use of their photograph taken just after Eddie scored a two point conversion just moments before his near fatal injury. A special thanks to Steve Brown for his photograph on the back cover.

I am grateful to Joe Sabah and members of the Colorado Speakers Association for encouraging me to write this story. Thanks to Mike and Brenda Staab for their encouragement and attention to detail.

My friends, thank you for your help in editing my writing: Loretta Bocast, Justin Bell, Peter Droege, Sue Foster, Peter Galmish, Mel Hilgenberg, Herrick and Lynne Lidstone, Peggy McKay, John and Rosemary Priester and Sister Catherine Erger from the English department at Machebeuf High School in Denver.

Thanks to Coach Bill McCartney, of the University of Colorado, for recruiting Eddie and Tom, for his prayers and support and for writing the foreword.

Special thanks to Father Bob DeRouen S.J. for being our friend and spiritual strength.

Many thanks to the volunteers who helped Eddie; especially Claudia McAdam and Tom Stock who have worked with him for eighteen years.

To the people of Littleton, Colorado, thank you.

TABLE OF CONTENTS

Isaiah 38:19

A father to the children
shall make known
the truth.

Scripture clearly states Almighty God holds a man responsible for the spiritual temperature of his home. How does a man do this? How can every father meet this divine responsibility?

You're OK, Kid! answers this important question. I have learned, in working with men for several years, there are two qualities to look for in a man which distinguish "Godly Men." Ed Reinhardt Sr. scores at the top of his class in both—Humility and Resolve—one without the other is less than true fatherly leadership.

Humility has vulnerability and servanthood attached to it. This is a quality learned through submission and confession.

Resolve implies getting up off the ground and back into the game. It is an unrelenting, persevering spirit. Fresh fire comes out of it daily.

This is how Ed Jr. played football and how Ed Sr. responded to his son's extraordinary misfortune. With humility and resolve.

Together they turned adversity into good fortune.

This book can transform your home.

—**Coach Bill McCartney**,
University of Colorado 1982–
1995, Founder of Promise Keepers

xi

Our Final Therapy Session

*O*ur umpteenth marriage counseling session, Thursday, September 13, 1984, was nearing the end of the hour. I looked down at my watch to be sure my time was the same as the therapists' clock on the wall just behind my head. Therapists have a way of looking directly at you and at the same time seeing their own clock, which tells them exactly when the session will be over. I wanted to use the last five minutes to tell them Pat and I were wasting our time and I wouldn't be back again.

I was angry about the time and money we had spent in this office, and others like it, trying to keep our marriage together. Over and over, we discussed the areas which kept our lives in such turmoil. My wife, Pat, and I simply came from opposite backgrounds. She grew up on a Nebraska farm as the oldest of six children. Her parents loved and educated their children. By their Christian example, they created the environment their kids needed to have healthy families of their own. On my father's side, there were three generations of divorce, desertion, promiscuity and an unwritten rule nobody stayed in the same place long enough to understand what the word stability meant. My dad, Floyd Earl Reinhardt, never owned a piece of property in his life. Why was I paying these people to tell us how we were different? Books like *Men Are From Mars, Women Are From Venus*

1

had not been written yet but, it was plain to anyone we came from different planets!

The therapists had shown us a diagram defining our family dynamics. Each member had a circle with his or her name written in it. My circle was off to one side of the page, all by itself. Pat and the six kids were grouped together on the other side of the page. I angrily denied the diagram was accurate and defended myself by explaining ways I was close to my children and Pat.

Early in our marriage Pat would say, "I don't know why you're even married; you don't seem to need me." Naturally, I resented this remark. It wasn't that I didn't want a close relationship, I just couldn't let go of my hurt or my fear of being deserted long enough to let anyone get close to me. I kept my distance from everyone. I wasn't going to suffer again what I had lived through as a child. From my time in therapy, I learned I had constructed walls around myself keeping me at a distance from other people. If I wanted to keep this marriage together, the walls had to come down.

I wasn't sure I could commit to anyone—commitment, intimacy, cooperation, interaction, honesty and openness were the buzzwords mouthed by the therapists. I wanted none of them.

"You came into this marriage but you left your luggage on the porch," Pat would scream in exasperation. "Come in and be here or get out."

Even after acknowledging my fear of commitment, I refused to acknowledge it was the problem. I rejected Pat's suggestion my behavior was the cause of our troubles. Over and over we were told by our therapists if I wanted to save our marriage, I needed to first determine what was creating my negative behavior, then I had to change. I had almost convinced myself the marriage was over because I would risk losing my wife and family before I would risk trusting anyone who could hurt me again.

Restlessness and my sense of discontentment were so strong, it seemed nothing could change me from the direction I was moving in. I felt my life had no purpose except to support my family. My work was only a means to earn money and the income was good. After struggling for twenty years working for a large corporation, I became self-employed and doubled my salary in two years; just in time to meet the needs of our six kids heading for college. Relieving my financial burdens with more money did not relieve my sense of hopelessness and despair.

Often I drove the streets of Denver making plans to move out and separate myself from my family. I daydreamed about living and working somewhere else and starting my life over again.

I was becoming obsessed with thoughts about my dad. In a few days I would be 51, the same age my father was when he divorced my mother some 32 years earlier. I thought about how much like my dad I was. I always reveled in the fact we had the same name and I was left-handed, like him. My Irish grandmother would always tell me, "Tubby, you look just like your dad." (Tubby was a nickname given to me by my dad because I weighed 50 pounds when I was three years old.)

Our session with the two therapists was about over. I was planning to jump in quickly and stop this nonsense. I could feel my breathing increase and my heart begin to beat faster. I knew a break in the conversation was only moments away and I was prepared. Before I could speak, however, Chuck (one of the therapists) interrupted my thoughts with a question, "Where are your sons playing football this weekend?"

Finally, we were talking about a topic I enjoyed! Suddenly I found myself expounding in detail on where each would play. We had five sons playing football and I loved bragging about them. I began by telling him, "Right after this session, Pat leaves for Lincoln, Nebraska, to meet up with our daughter Rosemarie. Together they will watch our oldest son, John, a nose tackle for the Nebraska Cornhuskers. I'm planning to leave in a few minutes for Boulder to have lunch with our second son, Eddie, before he travels to Eugene, Oregon, to play the University of Oregon Ducks."

Eddie was a sophomore tight end for the University of Colorado under Coach Bill McCartney. I crowed about how last week he had set a school record for pass receptions against Michigan State and was ranked second in the nation. I explained I would be back in Denver by four o'clock to watch our son Paul play for his grade school team. I completed the rounds by telling how I would be going to Tom's high school game Friday night. Then I knew I was bragging as I told them about our youngest son Matthew, who was just waiting in the wings for the chance to begin playing football at his grade school the next year.

I loved to tell about the successes of my children. Not many families in the United States had two sons playing major college football. I closed my monologue with, "What other family goes to twenty-five games a season to watch their own sons play football?"

Chuck and Sheila, our therapists, were unimpressed with my enthusiasm. When I finished, Sheila said, "Time's up. See you next week!"

"Damn," I thought, "I can't believe I didn't get the chance to call it quits!" "Damn," I whispered as I walked past the two of them and through the door, leaving them wondering what I was thinking. The ride down the elevator with Pat was quiet, not much different from hundreds of similar elevator rides.

As usual, we didn't have much to say to each other until we reached her car and only then to talk about the kids, their activities and our role in this weekend's happenings. The kids were the glue keeping us together. We worked well as a team when doing things for them. We would joke about our favorite child being the one with the biggest problem. We were good problem solvers for the kids, but we had a hell of a time settling our own disagreements.

As we leaned against the car, we went over the weekend plans once more. With so many football games each weekend, it had taken us an afternoon of scheduling back in August to decide who would attend which games. I had been back to Lincoln the previous week, so this week we switched. Pat would go to Lincoln to watch John. She planned to stop in Kearney, Nebraska, to visit her parents for the day, then drive the three hours to Lincoln before the game. Pat would spend Sunday with John and Rose and be back in Denver on Monday afternoon. Rose had just transferred from the University of Wyoming to Nebraska.

After going our separate ways, I drove to Boulder to meet Eddie at a Round-The-Corner restaurant for our favorite mushroom burgers. We talked about preparations for Saturday's game against Oregon. Those conversations may have been meaningless to him, but they relieved my anxiety about losing another game even if I wasn't playing. I had a hard time dealing with losing. Growing up, I believed winning was the only way to be accepted.

Eddie spoke about his week. He explained how he was recognized at the men's Buff Club and ladies Buffalo Belles luncheon for setting a school record in pass receptions. I knew he enjoyed those events, yet they did not disrupt his unassuming manner. "So you're going to Eugene. My experience with Eugene goes way back," I said sarcastically.

He chuckled and then became serious, "Dad, I'm sorry for what happened to you there."

"Forget it, Ed. That was a long time ago. What's important is you're going there to play a football game. I wish I could be with you."

After lunch we sauntered into the mall looking for the shoe store. I was dwarfed by this handsome, suntanned, brawny man— my son. He was turning the heads of the mall crowd without realizing his impact. I helped Eddie shop for dress shoes for his trip to Oregon, never dreaming of the upheaval which would take place in Eddie's life after we said goodbye.

The same afternoon, I was back in Denver by 3:30. I waited in front of the school for Matthew, who was 10 years old and in the fourth grade. Soon he came bouncing down the stairs, hardly able to keep his book bag on his shoulders in his rush to get to the car. His pleasant mood was obvious when he held out his hand and said, "Give me five!" Of all our children, Matthew looks most like me. At times it's eerie to look into his face and recognize the similarities we share. I hoped his early years would be better than mine. Whenever I thought about leaving my family,

I imagined his suffering the most. That alone should have been enough to discourage my thoughts of leaving. It wasn't.

Later, I watched Paul, then in the eighth grade, play defensive end for his team. Football was not Paul's first love. He was a genius for detail lost in a house full of jocks. A master at one-liners, he was sensitive and soft-spoken. His interests were in areas which challenged him intellectually—complex model railroad layouts, huge remote control airplanes and computers. For a long time he thought I expected him to play football. It was a relief for him to learn he was free to choose his own pursuits. Eventually, he traded his football cleats for ski boots.

It was nearly dark when the game ended. The warm car felt good after the cool evening air. The three of us knew the next stop was McDonald's for supper. We always went there after a ball game—and ball game or not, that's where we went when Mom was out of town. Mom being away was the best part of the weekend. When Pat was gone, structure dissolved and life took on a whole different meaning for us—we ate out, watched late-night television and slept in on Saturdays. Unless, of course, there was a ball game to watch on television. Ah, television! Television was something new for the Reinhardt family.

Just before leaving Columbia, Missouri to move to Denver in 1972, I decided the old black and white television set had to go to the city dump. Now, for the Reinhardt kids, going to the city dump was a positive experience. They found it more fun than a trip to the mall and I found it a lot less expensive. It meant a three-hour scavenger hunt for toys, old bikes and anything else they could imagine. We brought home more than we threw away, which was fine with me. Our most fun at the dump was a roofing shingle throwing contest. We applauded those who could hit the water below.

During their younger years I turned everything into a contest—from cake walks at the school carnival to wrestling matches on our living room floor—I pushed them to win. It made me proud to think games such as tossing shingles helped create their strong, competitive personalities.

The kids and I liked to enter the cake walks at their school picnics. With six players, including parents, we could monopolize the ten-station cake walk game and win most of the time. The kids loved winning and we needed the cakes.

Our daughter, Rosemarie, was always included in sports activities around home and acquired the same competitive spirit. She competed in, and won, many speech contests during grade school and was on the high school track team. Being the only girl placed her in a unique position. Being part of a family who were always talking about winning games helped her learn to compete. This drive earned her a journalism degree from the University of Colorado.

When it was time to toss the old TV down the embankment, we watched as it submerged in the water, out of sight and out of our lives. For the next twelve years we had no television. I rationalized it was best for the kids and easier for us to control what went into their impressionable minds. Deep down I knew I was the one addicted to the tube and getting rid of the old TV was the only way to deal with my problem. Left in the house, the TV would be another way to separate myself from my family—especially Pat.

As I sat there eating a Big Mac and shake, I felt like one of the kids. I realized how happy I was to be with them and was looking forward to five days away from my wife. I was not comfortable being around her anymore and I was much less tense when we were apart. We were moving further apart; our relationship was increasingly frustrating.

Fateful News

A light rain was falling over Denver that Saturday, September 15, 1984. I heaved the sheets of drywall from the pickup into the garage as cool raindrops splattered on my face. The change in weather was a welcome break since it had been exceptionally warm. The work I had to do in the garage was hot and dusty. By nine, all the wiring and electrical outlets were in place and the insulation was stapled between the studs. Drywall was next. While in college in Omaha, I had worked during the summer hanging and finishing drywall. I remembered my dad telling me about the plastering business he had during the depression to earn extra money for the family. I would not finish the work in the garage for two years.

I heard a noise in the kitchen, then saw Tom burst through the door leading into the garage. With typical abruptness and intensity, he shouted, "Dad! Dad! Will you take us to Laramie for a football game? It starts at one o'clock." Tom explained how the Wyoming Athletic Department had invited him to an Air Force–Wyoming game as a means to recruit him to play football for the University of Wyoming Cowboys. The mixture of love and loyalty I felt for Tom made the shift in priorities easy. "If Wyoming only knew how good Tom was," I mused, "they would send a limo for him."

Tom is our fourth child, then a high school senior. He played defensive lineman for Heritage High School in Littleton, Colorado. He was destined to play college football and had his sights on the University of Colorado, right beside his brother Ed. I recalled when John, Tom's oldest brother, was at Heritage High School, he'd held all the weight-lifting records across the board. One day while Tom was lifting in the weight room, he broke all but two of John's records, but without the official scorekeeper. A while later, when the scores were officially being kept, he was given only two records out of a possible eight listed. Tom didn't need to make his weight room accomplishments official. He knew in his heart what he could do and didn't feel the need to tell the world.

Tall and handsome with dark hair, Tom resembles Pat more than me. However, Tom and I are both left-handed, which makes us feel uniquely connected. We're both creative and enjoy each other's crazy sense of humor. I can relate to Tom's near-perpetual motion around home and at school. During his third grade year, we recognized Tom's inability to settle down and pay attention in class. With some intervention, Tom became an excellent student in high school and college.

We were getting a late start for the two and a half hour drive to Laramie and I knew I would have to rush to get us there before the 1 p.m. kickoff. Tom's high school buddy, Chris, was also being recruited so he accompanied us. By the time we left town, we knew we would miss the pre-game meeting with the coaches and other recruits. Halfway to Laramie, I learned Chris had to be home by 6:30 that evening. As we sped from Denver to Cheyenne on Interstate 25, irritated by the time crunch, I wondered why I had even agreed to go.

En route to the game, Tom, Chris and I reviewed their Friday night Heritage High School football game. I loved volunteering for the chain gang—moving the down marker chains at the sidelines. This gave me an inside look at the strategy and intensity of the coaches and players. I could watch the face to helmet butt chewing from the coach when a player screwed up. The fans seldom hear the crunching of helmets, which makes you wonder how the ball carrier ever gets up again, something I didn't like to think about.

The weather was cold and rainy east of the Continental Divide. About five miles west of Cheyenne, we came upon the worst traffic jam I'd seen this side of Chicago. Several people had been injured in an auto-truck accident. Traffic was being diverted back to Cheyenne, which intensified my impatience with the trip.

A man at a service station directed us to a highway which enters Laramie from the north. Finally moving west again, we reached the summit and started rolling toward Laramie. The highway took us into Curt Gowdy State Park where, without any warning, it became a dirt road. Again, we were crawling along outside of Laramie and Tom, expressing his frustration, started swearing about the situation. Hoping a few philosophical words would calm him down, I remarked, "Tom, isn't it strange how the road of life can change things for us when we least expect it?"

Tom mumbled, "Yeah, you never know, Dad."

It was hot and sunny in Laramie. Tom picked up the gate passes and we arrived at our seats for the beginning of the second quarter. After every score by Wyoming, a large cannon was fired. I've been to lots of football games and what I found exciting about this one was a flyover in formation of C-135 cargo planes from the Warren Air Force Base in Cheyenne. They roared in out of nowhere, appeared right above the stadium and were gone in an instant.

At the end of the third quarter we left the stadium and headed for Denver. I turned on the radio to listen to the Colorado-Oregon football game, hoping to hear something about Eddie and hoping Colorado was beating Oregon by a wide margin.

Colorado football was rebuilding after five losing seasons under the previous coach. The new head coach, Bill McCartney, had won only two games during his first season and four in his second year. This was the season to put them in contention for a bowl game. Eddie chose Colorado because of Coach McCartney.

He also had been recruited by UCLA, Stanford, California at Berkeley, Arizona State and Oregon. I, too, liked the new coach and felt like I could trust him with Eddie.

Bill McCartney played for the University of Missouri, then worked as an assistant coach at Michigan for nine years under the legendary Bo Schembechler. His recruiting techniques in our living room were awesome. His plan to create a nationally-ranked football program and his tenacious desire to form young men into useful adults, with an understanding of their need for a spiritual life, was everything I wanted to hear.

"Ball games are won in the living room," I thought.

I had to be quiet and let Eddie decide, all the while hoping he would play for Colorado. Coach Mac was definitely going to create a winning team—an idea I liked.

We were 85 miles north of Denver, just passing through Fort Collins. Colorado was behind by seven points. The announcer explained Eddie was alternating pass plays with the other tight end, John Embree, and working the ball down the field.

"It should be Eddie's turn next since Embree just came off the field," I thought. "Maybe Eddie will make the winning touch-down. They're getting close." Instead, they threw the ball to Victor Scott. "Tom!" I demanded, "Why did they throw the ball to Scott and not to Eddie?" The announcer instantly answered my question reporting, "There is some commotion at the Colorado bench. A player is down."

Every athlete's parent fears when a player is reported "down," that it's their child. For an instant I thought, "God, it can't be my son. It must be some other kid. It can't be Eddie! They'll report it's some other kid. I hope it isn't Eddie!"

"A player believed to be number 88, Eddie Reinhardt, has collapsed at the bench and medical personnel are gathering around Reinhardt." As Eddie's name was mentioned a third time, the game ended with Oregon beating Colorado 27 to 20.

In disbelief I listened intently to every word of the post-game coverage. I felt fear enter my stomach as I realized his condition could be quite serious. I'd been afraid many times in my life, by near car accidents or injuries to the kids, but now the terror was at my throat. I could hardly ask Tom what he was feeling. Finally, they announced Eddie was being taken to the hospital in an ambulance. Eddie's six-foot-seven, 235-pound muscular frame had always seemed invincible. I could hardly believe what was happening.

Gripped by panic, we moved through heavy traffic in Fort Collins at a snail's pace. I was out of control, screaming at the radio announcer, "What is happening to Eddie? Doesn't anyone know what the hell is going on?" By then I was traveling well over the speed limit and didn't care. We were still 60 miles from Denver when the announcer revealed Eddie was in the hospital where they were doing some tests and possibly preparing for brain surgery. It was finally reported Coach McCartney was with Eddie at the hospital and was trying to reach our home in Littleton.

I stopped in Loveland and raced to a pay phone. Paul answered. I tried to control my trembling voice, "Paul, has anyone called for us?"

"No, why?" he asked.

I tried to speak calmly, "Eddie was seriously hurt in Oregon during the football game and the coaches are trying to reach us." Paul was too stunned to answer. I continued, "If anyone calls from Oregon, tell them I'll be home in an hour and I will call them the minute I get there."

I jumped back in the car and sped off. Tom kept pleading, "Slow down! Be careful, Dad!" Tom, once a hyperactive child, reversed the roles as he attempted to bring restraint to my near hysteria. "God, will this trip ever end?" I yelled. I was losing my composure and an overwhelming fear of the unknown was taking over. "God, what is happening to Eddie?" I wept.

On the northern edge of Denver I called home again. "Paul, what's happening now?" "Coach McCartney called and wants to speak to you or Mom. He said Eddie is in the operating room." He added, "The house is full of people and the phone is ringing constantly."

"I'll be home as fast as I can."

Thirty minutes later I entered the house, greeted by a roomful of hurting and crying friends. Paul and Matt clung to me as I made my way to the phone. I knew I had to make the call but the possibility of hearing the worst paralyzed me.

It was like the gates of Hell had opened and all the worst things imaginable might be going on in Eddie's body—and of all places, in Eugene, Oregon? "Why Eugene?" I wondered. Soon I was listening to Coach McCartney explain Eddie was in the operating room having a blood clot removed from his brain.

"The operation will last another hour and Eddie might not survive. Get out here as soon as possible," he advised grimly. I hung up the receiver and reached out to hold my sons and began to cry. "This is the time for us to all be strong and pray for Eddie," I said. I repeated my conversation with the coach to those gathered and told them I had to leave for Oregon.

The phone call to Pat was nearly impossible for me to make. I knew she, John and Rosemarie would have gone out to eat after the game before returning to John's apartment. After several attempts and just before I had to leave for the airport, I finally reached John. I began by telling John the terrible news. At the same time, I was beginning to feel emotions, causing me to scream remarks which totally confused him. "John, you know what happened to me in Eugene, Oregon, don't you? I lost my Dad there. I can't lose Eddie there too!" I sobbed. "Why is this happening to Eddie in Eugene?" I repeated over and over. "We're going to lose him, John! We're going to lose him!" By then John was crying and telling me to settle down. I couldn't stop talking. He interrupted me to say, "Mom just walked in. Here she is."

I began to tell Pat about Eddie as best and as quickly as I could. "Call Coach McCartney right away at Sacred Heart Hospital in Eugene. I have to leave for the airport right now."

"Is Eddie still alive?" she demanded. "You've got to tell me the truth before you leave the house. If he is dead, I have to hear it from you! Is he still alive?"

"I am telling you exactly what I heard from Coach McCartney. As far as I know, as of ten minutes ago, he is in surgery now and he is alive. I have to leave for the airport now. I have to go, Pat.

You'll have to figure out how to get to Oregon as fast as you can! Patricia, I love you!" After I hung up the phone, I thought for a moment about what I had just said to Pat. The reality of telling Pat I loved her stayed with me for a long time after that phone call. I realized then, there was too much at stake to leave my family. Thoughts of leaving meant nothing. We were in danger of losing our child. My children were everything to me. I was there during their births; for the last two I was in the delivery room coaching Pat when they were born. Nothing was more important to me than the kids.

After hanging up the phone I was comforted to see my friend Nelse Hendricks standing in the kitchen. The more I expressed my fear of losing Eddie, the less he said and the more connected I felt to him. I asked him to make plane reservations for me and he did. When I asked him to take me to the airport, he said he had made reservations for two and he was going to Oregon with me. His strength and composure gave me a feeling of relief. I felt secure in the fact someone was caring for me. "God," I thought, "how much I need help!" Nelse Hendricks was the perfect gift from God for me then and during the years to follow.

Heartbreak in Oregon—Again

*N*else and I, along with his brother-in-law, Jerry Smith, started out the door for the airport. I hardly had time to say goodbye and felt torn leaving the children as they stood at the door surrounded by our friends. I knew they were confused about what was happening to Eddie and frightened he might not live. All they heard was his brain was injured, he was in surgery someplace far away and I had to leave them to be with him. I could barely imagine what they were feeling.

Eddie was special in the lives of Matt and Paul. It wasn't unusual to walk by their bedroom and see Eddie talking to them about athletics or schoolwork. I was thankful there was someone in the family who could answer their math questions! Eddie had the heart to take time with them and always encouraged them to do better. His behavior with his siblings didn't surprise me. It was his way—always looking out for others.

Jerry pulled away from the curb and we headed for the airport. My head was pounding with thoughts of Eddie.

What is happening in that hospital? Could he possibly be dead and I don't know it? I pleaded, "Oh God, don't let me even think about that!" I imagined Pat, John and Rosemarie in Lincoln, trying to get to Eugene. "God knows how it's going to work out," I thought. Again, I pictured leaving the kids on the front porch and tried to block the image from my mind because I couldn't do anything about them. Deep down I knew what I was trying to avoid. I knew I would have to face the thought eventually, I just wasn't ready yet. Remembering my connection with Eugene some 32 years before was too frightening.

I considered bringing it up to Nelse and Jerry, thinking it might help take my focus away from thinking about Eddie and leaving the kids. What would I say? "Hey, you guys, did I ever tell you about the time I had to testify at my parents' divorce in Eugene? Now I'm going back again. Wow! Isn't that something?" I decided it shouldn't come out that way. If I let myself start, it would come out of me like a hurricane. Nelse and Jerry wouldn't have any idea what the hell I was talking about. I wanted to ask them, "If this was going to happen, why didn't it happen during the game in Boulder last week or at Notre Dame next week? Why Eugene?"

I decided I just couldn't talk to them about it tonight. Though I was feeling half crazy about it myself, I had to stifle it for a while.

My behavior in the car fluctuated between outbursts of crying, begging God to save Eddie and asking Nelse and Jerry questions about Eddie neither of them could answer. I'm sure my sudden outbursts of rapid-fire questions about brain surgery and recovery frightened them. I couldn't stop rambling. In fact, the less they said, the more I felt safe to express my fear of losing Eddie. They knew there was a possibility he could be gone by the time we reached him. Their silence was a great gift to me then, as I cried out about my son, his situation and the harsh realities ahead of me.

We said goodbye to Jerry outside the terminal. Our plan was I would go right to the gate to be sure they held the plane while Nelse went to buy the tickets. I arrived at the gate as they announced the final call for the flight to Portland. We had decided earlier we would rent a car for the two-hour drive from Portland to Eugene. On the plane we were seated together but said nothing to each other for a long time. I knew if I opened my mouth, I would begin to choke up and cry and I didn't want to cause a scene. I looked over at Nelse several times and his expression assured me everything was under control. For once, it felt good to know someone else was in charge and looking after me. How many years had it been since I'd felt some relief from the responsibility of taking care of myself, as well as seven dependents? More and more I felt the peacefulness of letting go of the reins, knowing someone was there to carry the load, if only for a little while.

"Why doesn't this damn plane leave, Nelse?" I asked, in a loud and abrupt voice, partly crying and again feeling out of control. His strong, quiet voice assured me we would be leaving soon. The people around us looked startled. As I noticed them looking over at me, I had the feeling they thought I was acting strangely. They probably thought, "Great, all we need is a crackpot to listen to all the way to Portland." My actions didn't disappoint them as I kept shifting in my seat and rubbing my face. It was after nine o'clock and the other passengers were settling down. I was still jumping around in my seat like a little boy.

The attendant walked to our row and asked to confirm our names and destination. It seemed the crew had been alerted to see we made the flight. Nelse had purchased the tickets in his name and they were still waiting for passenger Reinhardt to arrive at the gate. Problem solved, the plane headed toward the runway. We were on our way to Oregon.

I tried to regain my composure as the plane departed. I began asking Nelse the same questions over and over again. He only looked at me, again making me feel safe and relieved. Thoughts of every kind were flying through my head as I lay back and closed my eyes. I pictured Eddie in surgery surrounded by doctors and nurses, all working to save him. "If they only knew him," I imagined. I've been reluctant to accept the kindness of strangers but nothing made me feel better than when someone was kind to one of the kids.

In my mind, I was telling Eddie how fast I was trying to reach him and begging God over and over to spare his life. "How could we ever live without him?" I cried. "Lord, please don't let him die." Still, I wondered how Pat would ever get to Eugene. I thought about Matt, Paul and Tom at home and all the people in our house when I left. I was sure the neighbors would make a plan to take care of the boys until relatives could come to Denver to be with them, but who? *I* wanted to be there with them. I reasoned the three older kids would understand this tragedy better and could deal with it more easily. I felt sad none of us would be there to comfort them.

Pushing the seat back, I tried once more to settle down and relax. My head was spinning. Will Eddie survive? Will he live another day? What do I know about brain injury and brain surgery? Again the question about Eugene. . . why there? Thinking about it brought too much pain. My impatience for any kind of an answer was driving me wild.

I couldn't concentrate on anything and surely I wouldn't hear an answer if I tried to listen. The question of going back to Oregon seeped into my thoughts again, only this time I let the idea in with a little less fear. I asked the Lord for an answer. "Please God, why do I have to go back? I'm afraid to go there. I've tried to forget about my bad experience there for so many years." About all I remembered of Oregon was seeing two large signs. One was a neon sign reading "EUGENE HOTEL" below our sixth-floor hotel room. The other sign read "UO," for University of Oregon, in huge white letters made out of rocks. This sign was clearly marked in my mind because at the time I was attending UO, University of Omaha. For 32 years I had repressed many memories of that first visit to Eugene and would return to the very city, where I experienced a tragedy in my own life, to be with my son who was critically injured and so close to death.

What about Eddie? What about Pat trying to get to Oregon? What about my kids at home? What's going to happen to us all? I paused, telling myself to relax and listen. I had never been in a mess like this. I thought I was in control of everything and could solve my own problems, but everything was out of order, nothing was working for me anymore. I was sure I was going crazy. Thank God I wasn't alone. My friend, Nelse, was sitting there quietly with a peaceful look, his eyes closed.

There was nothing to look at out the window, so again I quieted my mind to listen. "Edward, you have to go back for your answer; you have to go back through it all and search for the answer to your question if you want this accident to have any meaning for you." That thought remained with me for a long time.

I would spend a lifetime searching my past to find the sense of order I needed before being able to understand the purpose for my life. It seemed as if I couldn't get anything started until my past life was in some kind of order. The order I needed always centered on my dad. "If that relationship were in order," I thought, "I could move forward with my life and the road ahead would be brighter."

In my airplane seat, I was taken back to all the roads I had followed in my life. I found it pleasant for a moment to think about my grandmother, Bessie Rotherham, and the Old Hopkins Road near my birthplace of O'Neill, Nebraska. O'Neill is 185 miles northwest of Omaha and I had hitchhiked those miles many times just to get away from the city and the sadness of growing up in Omaha when my dad was working away from home. My grandparents had a farm in the middle of the Sandhills of Nebraska. The farm's openness was my playground and, as I grew older, I was able to help with the haying, tending the livestock and other farming chores. Eventually the farm became an escape for me. I was big and strong and my grandfather taught me how to operate the horse-drawn farm equipment. It never seemed to be work for me as much as it was playing with grown-up farm toys. Once they started using tractors for power, my interest dwindled and the fun was gone. When I was a little boy, I often imagined this farm was the place my dad talked about us having. He would say, "Someday, Tubby, we will live on a ranch of our own. . . somewhere out west in the mountains. We'll have horses and cattle. You can have a horse of your own to ride out to bring the cattle home." "Somehow," I thought, "I am going to make my part of his dream for us come true."

Old Hopkins Road was the way from the farm to O'Neill. It was named after an old homesteader, Roy Hopkins, who owned the land on either side of this two-mile stretch of dirt country road. It was narrow with only enough room for one car and, in the summertime, the road was covered with a natural canopy of trees and heavy underbrush at the sides. Every Sunday morning during the summer, I would ride the 20 miles to St. Patrick's Church in town, sitting behind my grandparents on a small wooden bench in their 1939 Oldsmobile Coupe. I liked to sit behind my grandmother and loved to listen to her stories of life as a girl growing up in Scranton, Pennsylvania. I liked the stories about her father working in the coal mines. "It's the hardest coal in the world," she would say. I later learned hard coal burns longer, which obviously was her point.

Grandma's father, Poppa, decided a mining life was not really a healthy one for his sons to have and chose to move the family west. Grandma told about their move to Nebraska in the early 1880s, building their home before winter, homesteading and the terrible blizzard of 1888. I listened to many stories on that bench and every story finished with a happy ending, which always made me feel good. Her optimism and her great pride were never defeated and she never ended her stories with sadness or disappointment for me to carry away.

The nearer we got to Old Hopkins Road, the closer I would nudge her because I knew the road would get darker under overhanging trees until we reached the halfway point. Only then could I see the small light at the end of the road which would begin to turn the darkness back into bright sunlight. My grandma sensed I became frightened each time we drove through this part of the road. I believed she saved the best part of her stories for this stretch of the road to draw my attention away from the darkness outside. So without fail, just before the halfway point, Grandma would say, "Don't look back, Floyd Edward! Look at the light at the end of the road." I watched the little light ahead grow bigger until we were in the clearing again and the sun was shining brightly. Coming out of the darkness always made me feel good.

For a long time I was told not to look back until I wondered why and became curious about what was happening behind the car. During the next few trips down Old Hopkins Road, I just sat on the bench listening to Grandma, dying of curiosity, wondering what was going on behind me that I shouldn't be seeing. Finally, following church service one Sunday, I decided to quickly take a look during the drive home. I felt nervous and excited at the same time but was determined to look back.

As usual, Grandma was right. The moment I looked out the rear window, I became frightened by the sight outside. The movement of the car created a vacuum as we moved forward and the wind was sucking the low hanging tree limbs and bushes against the rear window. The leaves were hitting up against the window and what appeared to be a monster was trying to reach in and grab me. I snapped my head back toward Grandma and nearly bumped her head.

I wanted to crawl over the seat and into her lap or just hold onto her neck until we were clear of this road. Suddenly I realized this was not the proper way to approach my grandmother, who seemed so refined and proper in her colorful summer dress and church hat. All I could do was lean a little closer to her face and say something to hide my fright so she wouldn't detect from my movements I just had the hell scared out of me. "You sure do smell good, Grandma," I said. She responded, "You're a good boy, Floyd Edward." "And here I am, looking back again," I thought. "I don't want to do it!"

The Early Years With Dad

J've heard it said some folks grow up in a house with four rooms and a bath. My first recollection of our house was one room and a path. In fact, it was little more than a small cabin my dad built for my mother and me. During the first few years of my life, I felt like an only child because my four older siblings were away at boarding school. Occasionally, I would see them around on holidays and during the summer. Even when they were home, they stayed in an old deserted two-story house behind the cabin, owned by some distant relatives who let Dad build our cabin on their property. It was 1938 and I was five years old.

Dad worked for the Holt County Department of Roads in the small town of Atkinson, located in north central Nebraska on the eastern side of the Sandhills. He was in charge of road maintenance and was responsible for keeping the roads graded, the snow plowed and the equipment in good working order. His shop was on our property, so I could be near him almost all the time. All the machinery was parked in the area near the shop and our cabin. Dad didn't mind living so close to his work, since his whole life centered around his work and no sacrifice was too great to get the job done to his satisfaction. His need to perform well for his employer was a great motivating force which provided him with praise and recognition. He was a good worker and an excellent employee.

My earliest memories of life were times when I was physically close to my dad. I clearly remember those times during the next two years of my life when I was sitting on his lap or he was carrying me in his arms or I was hanging on to his shoulders. He became so much a part of my life, nothing else mattered to me but him.

I remember when he took me along in the road grader to work on the dirt road leading to Stuart. He sat me on his lap and let me work the levers and the steering wheel of the big yellow machine. This experience put me in awe of the great power he had and I believed he could do anything.

When I took control of the machine, I experienced just a little bit of this power and I loved him even more for letting me share it with him. During those times, I felt like I was the only person in his life and I didn't want to lose this moment or share it with anyone. I wanted nothing ever to come between us and would do anything to keep it that way.

In winter I rode with him in the snowplow. We traveled south of Atkinson toward Amelia in the morning and returned in the afternoon. We stopped in Amelia at the local bar for lunch. My dad had a beer and I had a soda. He sat me right up on the bar and told all the guys I was his son. He would brag about me and tell them how well I could drive the truck and plow the snow. I sat on the bar, just taking in all this attention and loving him more than anything.

Summer evenings he would often take me over to the gravel pits to go swimming, just the two of us. We would swim out to the little island and play in the sand like a couple of kids. We built sand castles and sometimes he would bury me in the sand. As we left the island, he would tell me, "Hold onto me and don't let go." So, night after night, I assured him I would hold on and never let go of him.

The days when Dad was away working were lonely. I had to play in the house or the shop by myself waiting for him to come home. One afternoon, Dad came home and couldn't find me anywhere around the shop or the cabin. He searched frantically in the machinery, around the outbuildings and down around a ditch which was usually full of water. Dad was nearly hysterical when he decided to look once more back around the machine shop. He found me sitting up against the shop door which led to the back room of the garage. I had fallen asleep waiting for him to come home.

Electricity was not a luxury we enjoyed in our cabin. We had an icebox which used a fifty-pound block of ice to keep things cool. One Sunday afternoon, as I opened the compartment door, the ice started to slide out and before I could close the door, the block of ice knocked me down and landed on my knee.

My dad thought my leg was broken so he carried me six blocks to the doctor's house. At first I felt shy about being so close to Dad. Six blocks is a long distance to be carried. I could feel his body moving along the dirt road and I began to anticipate his next step and moved myself along with him. I could smell his body as he began to sweat from the hot summer afternoon. As my shyness dissolved, I looked up at his face, only a few inches away and could see his ruddy complexion and dark beard. I knew he cared for me by his determination to get me to the doctor. This awareness removed any pain I felt from my injury. The fullness of my dad's love was always obvious to me by the closeness I experienced with him during those early years. I don't remember him expressing his love for me verbally as much as I remember our physical closeness.

Memories of my mother in my life then are vague, although, eventually we became good friends and even attended college together. The mental pictures I had of her fit into three memories. Frequently, my mother took me to church. As much as I wanted to be with my dad, I was fascinated by the calmness I experienced kneeling next to my mom at Mass. Any religious training I received came from Mom and my grandparents since Dad wanted no part of going to church. My love for God would begin to grow from those early visits to church.

Another experience I had with my mother was during the birth of her sister's son, Matthew. Mom drove the 25 miles to

O'Neill to care for my Aunt Helen. Throughout her life, I watched my mom looking out for others, giving of her time and generosity.

I remember how she saved me from an invasion of ants which crawled up my shorts when I was playing outside in the dirt. It seems I sat down to play over an anthill and it wasn't long before I ran in the house screaming from the bites. She quickly brushed them out of my pants.

I believe the fewer memories we have of someone or some event, the greater the impact they make in our lives. Recollections of my parents from this period of my life stand out like a neon sign and I cherish each one.

My dad's job with Holt County ended rather abruptly in 1939. Although he had been recommended to be county engineer for Garfield County, the next county over, a Nebraska law was passed in 1938 mandating all engineers had to be college graduates. Since Dad quit school after the seventh grade, he was not eligible for the job. Dad was not one to hang around where there was little chance for advancement. The time I had with my dad was coming to an end as he began to look elsewhere for work. For the first time, I experienced life with Dad away from home and soon learned what it felt like without him. I know my mom cared for me but it didn't relieve the sadness and loneliness I felt without my dad. It was a scary time for me and a time of waiting.

A new construction job in Norfolk, Nebraska, brought the family back together. My four older siblings were living at home again. During the time alone with my parents, I'd had all their attention. However, upon the return of my brother and three sisters from boarding school, I became just the fifth child with little attention from anyone. The construction job ended after six months and Dad was on the road again looking for work. He spent the winter in Oklahoma, then moved on to Chicago.

Christmas of 1940 was tough for our family. Dad sent a check home for fifteen dollars and my mother sent five dollars back to him for expenses. With little money for Christmas, Mom packed us up and took us to her parents' farm where we had plenty to eat. Somehow she even scraped together a few presents for us.

During that tough year, my older brother John worked in an ice cream parlor for fifty cents a night and gave his earnings to Mom. While we were in school, Mom repaired coal sacks for five cents each to pay for coal for the furnace. I wasn't as aware of the hardships as were the older kids. I was going to school and spent my time waiting for Dad to come home so we could be together again.

One night in the spring of 1941, we heard a knock on the door and there was Dad. He was excited about a new construction job working for Peter Kiewit and Son Construction Company. Kiewit was building a large military complex south of Omaha called Martin Bomber Plant, then Offutt Airbase.

We talked and talked before finally going to bed. Mom was visiting her parents on the farm so I got to sleep with Dad. It felt like heaven having him home and I was able to feel once again how much he cared for me. I was seven then, the youngest in the family, and I was beginning to understand some things: My name was Floyd, not Tubby; I was named after my dad; and I was left-handed like him. I believed I was special to him and he liked me more than my sisters and brother because I was so much like him. We shared a closeness unlike the others.

My father's need to be on the move was becoming obvious to me as I grew older. I was told he had not known his father and had been on his own and living away from home since he was 14.

His mother eventually remarried and the older man didn't especially want kids around. Dad soon got the message and, when he turned 14 and was old enough to go to work, left home. He worked on the railroad in South Dakota loading gold bars from the mines onto freight cars. He worked as a cowboy on Wyoming ranches and broke horses for the army during World War I at Fort Robinson, in northwest Nebraska. He homesteaded in New Mexico and drove cattle in Texas and Colorado. After his stepfather died, Dad returned to Omaha and worked as a construction laborer. That's when his maverick lifestyle came to an end, at least for a while.

In 1923, Dad met a beautiful young Irish farm girl named Margaret—whom he called Maggie—from O'Neill, Nebraska. Mom's family background was almost the opposite of Dad's, paralleling those of Pat's and mine. Mom was a daddy's girl, too. Her father was a strong husband for my grandmother and a good father to their seven children. Mom's siblings all grew up on the farm and worked to help the family and each other. Their lifestyle was foreign to Dad. He was friendly toward my grandfather but rebellious toward his authority. Dad was always suspicious of anyone trying to control him. I think Mom found excitement in Dad's worldly background and was attracted to his lifestyle.

During my parents early life together, Dad was working as a painter for the Ford Motor Company in Omaha. The plant soon closed and moved to St. Louis, Missouri. Dad and Mom moved with the company and he continued working for Ford until massive layoffs took place there in 1930. He found work in construction and learned the plastering trade until he was able to move the family back to my grandparents' farm in Nebraska. With two kids and twins on the way, it was decided being close to her family would be best for Mom. Three years after my twin sisters were born on that farm, I was born at home on September 11, 1933, the fifth of six children.

A year after I was born, Dad started working for the state of Nebraska in Atkinson. Dad worked long days and weekends to support the family, earning about $100 a month. During the early '30s, his hobby of building and repairing whiskey stills became another source of income. The Prohibition Era, from 1920 until 1933, forbid the manufacture or sale of alcoholic beverages. The era became famous for violence and a wild way of life which helped give the decade its nickname, the *Roaring Twenties*. His close calls with the sheriff made for many exciting stories. Only once were my parents faced with the law at our door. Dad was able to stall them long enough for Mom to drain the bathtub of whiskey. Dad liked plenty of adventure and excitement in his life.

My father's problem was he couldn't find balance. He was either so strict no one could endure him, or so permissive when he was working away from home, he was out drinking and chasing around.

He always had to be the boss and Mom liked his ability to take charge at home. He tolerated no monkey business from his employees and less from us kids. He respected employers who gave him the freedom to use his own creativity and authority to direct his workers. His hard work and ability to get the job done were respected. Lucky was the employer who recognized his needs. Dad would work under any conditions, travel anywhere to work and sacrifice everything to get the job done.

Little did I know of his work habits then, but someday I would become their victim and would suffer because of it. He had an enormous emotional need for security and self-esteem and a need to discover his own masculinity. He found it all through his work life.

The Peter Kiewit Construction Company was just the employer to meet those needs. Kiewit was a large road and bridge building company headquartered in Omaha with offices throughout the country. The Kiewit Building was six blocks from our house. Most of the company's work was road-building for federal and local governments. When World War II began, Kiewit moved to building military bases throughout the country and around the world. Kiewit started in Omaha in 1909, about the time a French company was designing the famous Letourneau earth-moving machine. This machine would be able to move and grade more dirt in a day than other machines could move in a week. They won a lot of contracts in Nebraska betting the machines would be built and ready to use when the work started.

The company and my dad were a perfect match. Dad could operate every piece of equipment Kiewit owned and bragged he could repair any breakdown in half the time as any of the company's regular mechanics. He was on the job early, stayed late and expected the same from the employees working on his crew. He could recognize a good worker quickly and fire a loafer in an instant without remorse. His attitude was, "if you don't work with my degree of intensity, you don't keep your job because there are three other guys waiting to fill your shoes." It didn't take Kiewit long to recognize his work ethic. They primed him with raises and soon promoted him to job foreman.

For the war buildup, many airbases were being built, especially on the West Coast. Kiewit was awarded most of the contracts and was moving men to work those jobs. Dad was soon managing the operation of new machinery called Barber-Greene which spread hot asphalt. The Barber-Greene took the mixed oil and material from trucks and spread them directly onto the road surface, making a better road in half the time.

The job with Kiewit at the Martin Bomber Plant lasted for several more months before Dad was relocated to another site. The family had moved several times in the past and would go right along with Dad to the next job. No one ever thought another plan might be in store for us.

I was in the third grade and obedient and respectful of Dad's authority. I worshiped him and still tried to be with him as much as possible. I always quit playing with my friends after four in the afternoon so I could go to the bus stop and wait to walk him home. There I would sit in an apple tree to get a better view of the bus coming down the street. The second I could see the bus, I ran toward him with a hug and reached for his black lunch box. Then, hand-in-hand, we walked home. Dad was the most important man in my life and I would do anything to please him. He kept after me to do well in school and I tried my best to get good grades for him. Always, for him.

School was never easy for me. Today, I would be classified as having a learning disability. I was a "hyperactive" boy (the old word for Attention Deficit Disorder) as I had difficulty controlling myself in class. I got into lots of trouble and this behavior was reflected on my report card.

I actually remember being tied to a chair with a rope in kindergarten because I couldn't sit still. In the first grade, the nun passed out holy cards to anyone who behaved. I received only one card during the year because I fell asleep in class. No one at home recognized those problems nor helped to solve them.

I began to see a change in my dad. He was getting short-tempered and growing distant from all of us. Being the youngest, I was the last to experience his harsh rules around home. He was very restrictive with my siblings and demanded they work part-time to pay for some of their own needs. He thought athletics and other after-school activities were a waste of time. My brother John quit his high school basketball team because Dad yelled at him for not being home for dinner. Dad had few interests aside from his work and thought we should be the same.

His attitude continued to worsen. I tried harder to be good and began to stay away from him. One morning the alarm clock failed to ring and he was late for work. He threw the clock down the basement steps and the thing kept ringing even after it broke into several pieces. Those outbursts of anger frightened me. One night in the car I asked him for some popcorn. He yelled at me and I began to cry. I thought my world was falling apart and I didn't understand why.

When I was in the third grade he caught me trying to smoke a cigarette in the park with my friends. He brought me inside and told me to smoke in front of my grandparents, some aunts and uncles and the rest of the family. He made a joke out of it and everyone laughed at me. I was humiliated and heartbroken.

About the same time, I brought home a report card with low marks in deportment, for bad behavior in school. Dad took his belt and hit me so hard my twin sisters ran to Mom to beg her to make him stop beating me. Such negative experiences with my dad caused me to wonder for many years if I had been the one who caused him to leave home.

I believe the unconditional love I felt for my dad ended after those events. I know some of my emotional growth and psychological development ceased after he left the family. Any masculine influences I would experience from then on would come from uncles, fathers of my friends, teachers, employers and other men I would meet—some good and some bad. Some I would trust and some I wouldn't but, after Dad's departure, I was suspicious of every man I met. A man had to prove to me he was trustworthy. I learned quickly I'd better take care of myself because no one else would.

Peter Kiewit didn't move a man and his family in 1942 as gently as they do today. If you were transferred today, they would call a moving company, give you a month's salary and pay for the family to stay in a motel. What they said to my dad in 1942 was, "Reinhardt, if you want a job, meet us in Casper, Wyoming. We'll hold the job open for one week. Any longer than that and you're out of luck." That's all it took. My dad was gone.

That sunny spring morning of 1942, Dad and a fellow worker started out driving to Casper, where they would go to work for Kiewit building an airbase for the military. Eventually, he was moved up to the Aleutian Islands to continue building military installations for the government during World War II. His friend lasted four weeks in Casper and returned home to his family. He told us he was unable to cope with a construction worker's life of living out of trailers on the job site and working seven days a week.

I thought about him settling down on the West Coast after the war. I thought about my mom and dad and my younger brother Jim and how it was when we said goodbye on the street corner of Broadway and Pearl in Eugene, Oregon, 32 years earlier. For a second time, I was afraid to make this trip to Eugene. I feared reliving my experiences in this city so many years ago.

I remembered myself as a 19-year-old college student in Omaha, trying to put my life back together and trying to make something of myself after losing my dad through the divorce. I thought about how my dream had ended abruptly in Eugene in February of 1952, when I stood in front of the judge in that courtroom to swear Dad did in fact desert my mother and us kids.

I could still hear the judge's final words ringing in my ears: "Divorce granted!"

Dad's Promise

Dad's departure in April of 1942 was so sudden and my attitude toward him was changing so much, I was confused and unsure of my feelings. On one hand it was a relief to have less tension in the house, but at the same time I had lost the person I loved the most. I felt very alone during the next several months. I didn't have the same closeness with Mom and my brother and sisters were older and busy with their own activities. I had few friends since I had not made time for anyone else but Dad. I spent a lot of time daydreaming about my early days with him, thinking about the little island where we played together.

I kept busy mowing lawns, cleaning yards and shoveling snow after school to earn spending money. My activities did not extend to my schoolwork and, without the fear of Dad's beatings, I did almost anything but homework. After the third grade, my grades were barely high enough to pass.

Early in the fourth grade I decided I didn't like my first name, Floyd, so I changed it and started using my middle name. I went up to Sister Mary Elizabeth and asked her, "Sister, how do you spell Edward?" As she spelled out E-d-w-a-r-d, I asked her not to use Floyd anymore. Years later I wondered what possessed me to make such a change in my life. I believe I had a need to separate myself from Dad and the name was a painful reminder of him. Edward was a more gentle name, one I could relate to. I learned about an English saint known as Edward the Protector. As it happened, "protector" was a role I would fill during the next several years.

Several months after Dad left home, my brother John entered the Navy and served aboard a landing craft in the South Pacific. My oldest sister, Rita, enlisted in the Marine Corps and was stationed in California. That left my mother, my twin sisters and me. During the fall of 1942, my mom had my sisters, Kitty and Bunny, or me walk with her around the park each evening. I didn't know then the exercise was prescribed for her pregnancy. Time with Mom became special for me because I began to feel her love in a new way.

The baby clothes pushed under her bed still did not give me a clue she was expecting a baby. I was told they were for my cousin, Billy Hynes, who was born six weeks before my brother. We welcomed James Anthony into our family that November and he delighted us all.

If I didn't realize I was the family protector then, I soon got the message from my relatives and friends. "With your dad and big brother gone, it looks as if you're the man of the family," was a remark I heard over and over. I got a lot of attention in this position so I worked even harder to become that man.

My own interests became secondary to the demands of the family and it took me many years to learn who I would like to become. I let the needs of the family dictate my decisions, so my purpose in life was not clearly defined. Money was always a major concern at home and, eventually, I identified this as my primary goal. Personal interests came second to the family's needs.

Several months after Dad left for Wyoming, I began to realize plans to move there with him were being discussed less and less at home and nothing in his letters made mention of us moving. I suspected he didn't want us with him.

Any talk about moving ended with his last letter from Casper. We learned the airbase runway was finished and his job was to load the equipment on railcars for a move to the West Coast. Although the federal government required prior permission for any train in the United States to be moved, Dad ordered the train to start moving early. He claimed a wartime priority shipping status, which allowed them to move construction equipment for military purposes. The train moved out of Wyoming and arrived in Seattle ten days early. Dad's gutsy decision was applauded by Kiewit. Soon he was working on an island off the coast of Alaska.

One day after school I had occasion to stand up for my dad's honor. I was with some of the boys in the neighborhood and we started talking about our dads, each taking a turn bragging about what our father did for work. I explained my dad was building military bases for the government in Alaska. This story outshone the others and I was feeling pretty good. One of the kids, whose dad had a less exciting job but was home with his family, blurted out, "Hey, Reinhardt, your old man ain't never coming home!" To an 11-year-old, those were fighting words. I ran to him and started a fight. He hit me right on the nose and the next thing I knew, I was lying on my back seeing stars with blood pouring out of my nose. Determined, I went back to him and we began to wrestle. I finally had him down with his hands pinned to the ground and thought, "Now what?"

My buddy standing next to us started yelling, "Hit him, Ed! Hit him!" By then I realized if I let go of one hand to hit him he could get loose and I would be in trouble.

So there I was, holding him to the ground, leaning to the side with blood flowing down my face, when my buddy finally yelled to me, "Well, bleed on him, Ed! Just bleed on him!" The fight ended with my sisters running to get my mother. I was satisfied having defended my father's honor.

I realized later I wasn't angry with the kid—I was angry about the truth. The thought of my dad never coming home had begun to sink in. As much as I tried to deny it, I believed it to be true. My feelings about Dad varied tremendously from one day to the next. If I thought he didn't love me or want to be with me, then I figured he was never coming home. If I believed he would come back, then I would daydream about our time together. My mind was never at peace about anything because everything in my life was connected to our relationship. I had to believe in him before I could believe in anything else.

Dad's letter and support check each month arrived from the Aleutian Island of Attu. He remarked briefly about his work. . . the weather, he wrote, with constant rain and fog, was as much a battle as the war being fought on some of the South Pacific islands. The crews worked in all kinds of weather and around the clock. Most contracts for military work were on a cost-plus basis. Costs were no issue for the government and Kiewit was certainly profiting. The demand by the military to finish jobs ahead of schedule propelled the men to work well beyond their endurance. Most of the work was done in darkness with men pushing themselves to their limits. The accident rate increased. Dad became one of those statistics when he stepped down from a machine after several hours on the job. It was dark and he didn't see a hole below him. He heard a snap, felt a sharp pain in his left leg and fell to the ground. Dad suffered a broken bone and was soon off the job.

Kiewit wanted my dad back on the job as soon as possible, so they offered to send him home during his recovery at their expense. He could go home for six weeks with pay, then go on to Chicago to the Barber-Greene Manufacturing Company for training on their latest asphalt spreader. He would then return to the island and train other operators. They had ordered several machines which would be delivered soon after his return. Dad took the assignment and we were notified he was coming home.

My joy was beyond imagination. His ten days of travel by train to Omaha couldn't go quickly enough for me.

Dad's attitude had changed completely since leaving two years earlier. He had a good job, steady income and seemed to have reached the level of stability he so desperately needed. He realized Kiewit officials trusted him enough to give him full responsibility and he wasn't going to let them down for any reason. The company instilled in him the power and control he desired. He was at peace with his work and was fulfilled. Family played no part in his satisfaction.

The six weeks Dad was home in 1944 would be among the happiest days of my life. His leg in a cast and able to move around only on crutches, he spent his days with Mom and me and my two-year-old brother, Jimmy. I spent every day after school with him and listened to stories of his adventures—places he had been, funny people he had met, crazy things his men did on and off the job.

Having Jim around the house all day was sort of a novelty for Dad. They had a constant teasing battle going on and Jim had lots of fun hiding the yardstick Dad used to scratch his itchy leg, which was encased in a cast up to his thigh. Dad tried to chase him around the house and Jim thrived on the extra attention. Dad was a great prankster, so they spent the days entertaining each other. Except for the afternoon he spent with Dad the day of the divorce eight years later, this short interval was Jim's only time with Dad for the next 29 years.

Before Dad's time at home ended, I felt the pain of his upcoming departure. He had changed so much and was so different from the cranky and short-tempered person he had been two years before. It probably wasn't the fact he had changed so much as it was he no longer felt responsible for his obligations at home. He seemed to be more like a visitor than a father and he knew he'd be living his maverick lifestyle again the minute the train left the station. I was able to convince myself he still loved me and told myself I was wrong to think he had just pulled out and left us.

The train for Chicago was scheduled to leave Omaha Sunday evening and we all planned to go to the train depot. Before leaving, Dad said he needed to go to the drugstore for cigarettes and asked me to walk with him. His cast had been removed and his leg was still weak and tender. The sidewalks were icy and he needed someone to watch for ice and to lean on when crossing the street. I was proud to be asked. I held his hand most of the way as we slowly and carefully walked the two blocks to the store. I wished the store was miles away as I never wanted that walk to end.

Dad began talking about living in the West. He described the beauty of the mountains and the beautiful scenery in Oregon and Washington and talked about how much he would like living there. Suddenly, he paused and then said, "Tubby, would you like to live on a cattle ranch in the mountains someday?" My whole body jumped with excitement at the thought of this arrangement. I thought of the summers on my grandparents' farm in Nebraska. Being out there was fun, but to live with my dad on our own land with horses and cows would be fantastic. Wow, this would be everything I ever wanted.

"Sure, Dad," I answered, "that would be great! I'd really like that." "Good!" He said, "Because someday we're all going to move out West and have a place of our own. I want us to live in the mountains on a ranch." Inside, I was screaming to myself how much I wanted that to happen. I wanted to say, "When?," but I was afraid to ask. I wanted to tell him how I was so anxious to move away from the loneliness I felt without him, how hard school was for me and how I didn't want to live with just the girls and brother Jimmy anymore. I was afraid to say anything.

Dad started talking again about moving out west, then promised me someday, after he returned from Alaska, we would have a ranch and all of us would be together again. Again, he told me I could have a horse and said we could raise cows. I was so overwhelmed by those words, by the time we got home my fears and the loneliness I anticipated about his leaving were gone. I believed I could handle anything for a while if I knew someday we would be together again.

The pain of saying goodbye to Dad was smoothed over by the promise he made to me that night. The picture he drew for me made my life seem easier to understand and accept. I thought, "If I just hold on and wait, soon I will be doing something I really want to do."

No real time frame had been mentioned during our talk that night. As my father boarded his train, I realized the only person who could make my dreams come true was gone again.

Picking Up the Pieces

*D*uring the next few years, I stayed too busy to notice any deterioration in my parents' relationship. I was too naive to realize a man away from his wife and family for several years was a problem. I never witnessed any expression of love between them and the thought of sex between them was even more foreign. I never even thought about Dad having lots of free time—alone. His letter continued to arrive each month with a check and a brief note about his location.

Nothing much was said about our move to the West Coast to join Dad. Occasionally, over dinner, we talked about him and whether he ever had any plans for us to join him. Mom seemed reluctant to just pack up and move out west without him knowing we were coming. With him working away from home all the time, she said we would be without him as much there as we currently were. With all four of her youngest kids still in grade school, she wanted to be certain there would be little disruption in our lives. Also, she didn't want to be so far away from her family since her parents and siblings played a big part in our support.

My studies in the Catholic school always seemed harder than the public school my friends attended. After barely completing the fifth grade and surviving the wrath of Sister Mary Damian, I thought I could finish grade school with little trouble. Staying after school, doing extra homework, being restricted from playing football and basketball, marching over to the pastor, bringing Mom to school to help settle down my behavior and cleaning up the cafeteria after lunch all became a way of life for me. I thought Sister Mary Damian hated me and took her anger and frustration out on me. However, during the fifth grade, she taught me to appreciate music and insisted I sing in the choir. I stayed after school for weeks just to learn Latin so I could become an altar boy. During the next three years as an altar boy, I felt very close to Jesus and experienced the kindness of our pastor, Monsignor O'Brien.

I breezed through the sixth grade with Sister Mary Colette, and the seventh with Sister Mary Elizabeth. I just believed I would sail through the eighth grade with Sister Mary Loretta and right into ninth grade when, unexpectedly, Sister Mary Loretta died. An eighth grade teacher and principal needed to be a good disciplinarian, so who did they replace her with but Sister Mary Damian! Surprisingly, the eighth grade was better with her than the fifth. Either she grew tried of trying or I had matured enough that we could get along and become friends.

Graduating from the eighth grade was a special day for me and my diploma was even marked "Special." Actually it meant I had to take summer classes in English and math or I would have to repeat the eighth grade. That was "Special!"

Sister Mary Damian never missed an opportunity to make me a better person, no matter how hard I tried to resist her efforts. I visited her many years later and her embrace was worth all the slaps on the hand it took to help me grow up.

The day after I completed the ninth grade in high school, I hitchhiked the 200 miles to O'Neill, Nebraska, where I was to spend the whole summer. I spent the first month in town with my cousins before moving to my grandparents' farm to work in the hayfield. I found kids in small towns had more fun than we had in the city, so I joined in and became part of the gang. We would go to the next town to play American Legion baseball or, if it was Saturday night, we would look for a fight. Sometimes we traveled over the same roads I traveled with my dad in the grader or the snowplow. For a moment I would try to recapture those feelings I had riding with Dad.

Day or night, we swam in the Elkhorn River just south of O'Neill, but Saturday nights were saved for Danceland, a local dance hall. I did my first serious drinking and smoking at Danceland, where there was more drinking outside than there was dancing inside. If we weren't drinking outside, watching a good fight was at least better than going through the embarrassment of asking a girl to dance inside. Besides, asking some guy's girlfriend to dance was a sure way of ending up outside in a fight.

My uncle Matt owned a beer tavern in O'Neill and the Nebraska Liquor Commission allowed minor children of the family to tend the bar and serve beer. I asked him if I could work in his tavern and he agreed. I would arrive early to clean up from the night before, sweep the bar and poolroom area, vacuum the pool tables and clean the five spittoons. The best part of the job was tending bar and listening to the old cowboys, some raised in the late 1800s, telling of their experiences working on cattle ranches in Nebraska. I envied them as I dreamed about my chances of living on a ranch someday with Dad.

I learned a lot that summer. I was free of any parental or school control and experienced a lifestyle much different from that at home. I had acquired a taste of the maverick way of life and I liked the freedom to do as I pleased. I liked the beer parties, playing baseball, talking to girls and, reluctantly, even learning to dance.

After the Fourth of July of 1948, the hay was ready for harvest and I moved onto the farm with my grandmother and my uncle, who operated the farm since my grandfathers passing a few years earlier. Being with them was always second best to living on a ranch with my dad. However, at night I would think about being in town with my cousins and raising hell around O'Neill. I had met a girl in town named Loraine. It was confusing trying to understand why I would rather be alone on the farm when I could be with her, going to movies and dances at Danceland.

Romantic interests aside, my love for the farm and working in the hayfields exceeded any notion of being back in town. My jobs were dictated by my uncle and I liked the challenges he gave me. I started with milking the half-dozen cows, feeding the calves and separating the milk. My uncle was daring enough to teach a city boy how to harness a team of two-thousand-pound horses to work in the fields.

He let me figure out how to operate a horse-drawn mower and hay rake. I thrived on the responsibility. All the local farm workers wore leather work gloves in the field. For me, my gloves were a symbol of my maturity first, and a means of protecting my hands second. Farmwork didn't seem like real labor for me that summer and the thought of the fun I was missing in town was seldom on my mind. I learned work was all about perseverance and, during that last summer on the farm, I matured a lot.

There were other things I experienced that summer I wished I hadn't. At nearly 15, my innocence from sexual experiences kept me a happy and easygoing kid. The world was a simple place for me. I didn't have many problems to solve until the night I awoke with someone in my bed. My grandmother's farmhouse had three bedrooms. Her bedroom was downstairs, my uncle's was upstairs and my room was opposite his. Sometime during the night I was awakened by a hand scrambling around near my underwear. I was shocked as I rolled over and quietly laid near the edge of the bed. It was my uncle. He moved closer and again tried to grab me. I got out of bed and just stood there while he lay there without moving. I didn't know what to do. I decided to leave the room and go to the stairway landing and lie down there, thinking he might go back to his room. I woke up the next morning and went back to my room, hoping he was gone.

Nothing was ever said about that night or the three other times that summer he came to my room attempting to fondle me. Each time I would get up and go downstairs. I hated my uncle for that. I felt dirty and confused and had no one to tell. I couldn't tell my grandmother and would never tell my mother. For thirty years, I thought the incidents were my secret, until I learned differently while attending another uncle's funeral. My older brother and three cousins were talking about this uncle and how they also woke up to find him in their beds.

I said to my brother and cousins, "You mean to tell me this happened to you guys and you never warned me about him?"

"Did he come to your bed?" my brother asked. "I thought everybody in the family knew about him." They all snickered when they realized I too had been threatened by his behavior. I felt disgusted and angry with my brother for a long time. I felt like he had deserted me by his silence. This event only reinforced my belief I had to be alert to the intentions of every man who came into my life.

I had come to the farm for five summers, but the summer of 1950 would be my last. Having all the hay stacked in the fields and the equipment repaired and put away for another year meant it was time to go back to high school in Omaha. Few things were as sad for me as the end of summer and leaving the farm. It didn't seem right so much fun had to be traded for the misery I felt in school. Even my weekly trip down Old Hopkins Road would be missed because I seldom looked backward. Instead I kept my eyes on the little light at the end of the road as it grew bigger and brighter. This was another lesson I was to use many times during the years ahead.

My feelings about leaving the farm changed dramatically after I met Donna in Typing 101 at the start of my sophomore year. I had to take the class over the following semester because I fooled around too much talking to Donna. It was even more painful when the teacher finally moved me to another desk. Repeating the class was a drag but learning to type served me well in school, the military and throughout my entire work life. Years later, at a class reunion, I learned Donna also flunked the class.

Donna was short, blue-eyed, blond and wore glasses. Her mother died when she was young so she was raised by her aunt and uncle. We talked a lot about our families and delighted in the fact she had a father and I had a mother. Her Aunt Helen and Uncle George liked me. I liked them and enjoyed being with their family. They worked in the packing plants of south

Omaha and one thing I remember is how they loved to eat. Each night after our date, they would insist I have a sandwich. It usually turned out to be a full meal and, of course, Uncle George would say, "Go easy on the butter, Ed. That's all we have 'til payday." Believing him, I would try to put the butter back on the plate, only to hear them break into laughter. Uncle George was a big part of my life over the next two years and I learned a lot from him. I think he viewed me as the son he never had.

First loves are usually unforgettable experiences because so many "first events" go along with a first love. There were also many fears I had to overcome in just getting acquainted and asking for the first date. After overcoming those obstacles, we shared movies and school events and lots of time together in school. I really wanted to kiss her and began wondering how and where. This urge was getting the best of me, so during a high school sponsored hayrack ride, I finally got up the nerve. We were buried deep in the hay and, after several mental attempts, I finally kissed her. Before the ride ended, I kissed her again. Only this time I reached out and took off her glasses before my lips touched hers. By then I could barely breathe. I wasn't sure what she thought about kissing me, but while saying goodnight on her front porch we kissed again; only this time Donna initiated the embrace. I was so excited after my first kiss I was barely able to keep myself from dancing and yelling all the way to the corner streetcar stop. The reality of not having my own car dampened my excitement a bit as I stepped onto the streetcar. Still, I rode home reeling in the memory of taking Donna's glasses off to kiss her.

The fun and closeness Donna and I shared over the next two years in school made up for all the unhappiness I was feeling at home. We made plans together for our future, as we both wanted to get married right out of school. We traded rings at graduation, attended all the parties and proms together and talked with some of our closest friends about getting married. I was having trouble committing to that decision, so we decided to wait awhile.

In the meantime, I decided to attend college. To earn enough money for school, my buddies and I took road construction jobs which took me out of town and away from Donna for the summer. Again I found myself free of any control and took advantage of my time away from home, school and Donna. I didn't write to Donna each week because I was out partying with my friends and getting acquainted with some of the local high school girls. "Was I just like my dad?" I wondered. Because of the instability I had in my family, I feared my marriage would end up just like my parents'. I just couldn't get married until my fear and uncertainty were gone. I told myself, and Donna, I had to have more time.

Divorce Granted

*J*t was obvious Dad's relationship with Mom was all but over. His support checks were coming less frequently then and seldom was anything written to Mom or us. Weeks and months would go by with little said about Dad. When letters did arrive, they were always postmarked from a different town or state on the West Coast. He had been promoted to job superintendent, which required him to travel more often.

My older brother John, who had worked with Dad for two years in Washington state, told me about the life road workers had and said he couldn't live like that anymore. John was mechanically inclined like Dad and a hard worker. He said they lived in a converted truck trailer on the job site. They worked long days and usually worked seven days a week. They seldom had time off and, when they did, it was spent washing their clothes and hanging around in bars. John tried to persuade Dad to come home to the family. Dad refused, ending their relationship for nearly 25 years.

When the sheriff delivered the divorce notice that September afternoon in 1948, the day before my sister Bunny's wedding, there was plenty of commotion around the house. The upbeat atmosphere surrounding the wedding preparations changed for all of us. We did our best to make it a happy day for Bunny and nothing was said about it to anyone outside our family. It had been over five years since any of us had seen Dad, so it didn't come as a big surprise when he didn't attend the wedding or respond to the invitation.

I was mostly frightened by the divorce notice. I didn't know anything about divorce since none of my friends' parents were separated or divorced. Wanting to be alone after I was told, I went to my room and lay on the bed for a long time. I was stunned and confused and really didn't know what to think. Finally, I decided living without a father after the divorce wouldn't be much different than before.

I was sad and disappointed with my mother and siblings because they didn't make any effort to keep the family together. Maybe I expected too much from them. I wanted someone to just do something.

From then on it seemed I couldn't make any plans or get anything started in my own life until I had some closure to my relationship with my dad. I thought about him constantly. If he would just come home, I could go on with my own life. "Maybe the divorce would end my belief Dad still cared about me so I could go on without him," I thought. My anger toward my dad began the day the divorce notice arrived. I had no other choice but to be mad.

In the early 1950s, the person who initiated the divorce proceedings had to have sufficient grounds; the courts would not authorize dissolving a marriage for frivolous reasons. Mom traveled to the West Coast twice to attend court proceedings and twice the court denied my father's request. Finally, realizing he wouldn't consider a reconciliation, Mom decided to file a countersuit for divorce on the grounds of desertion and the court date was set for February 23, 1952, in Lane County in Eugene, Oregon. Dad just happened to be working on a construction job in Eugene, so the hearing would be held there. Mom planned for me to go to Oregon to testify on her behalf. Dad was 51 and I was 19 at the time.

I was not doing well my first year in college at Omaha University and being gone for two weeks would only add to my problems. My professors didn't understand the necessity for my absence and they were indifferent toward my excuse. I really didn't care what they thought and my efforts in school reflected my attitude. At the end of the semester, I was asked not to enroll for the following year. As they put it, "Your grades are terrible and your attitude in class is even worse."

It took three days of traveling to get to Eugene by train. I had plenty of time to think about my first meeting with Dad after ten years. My little brother Jim, then nine, came with us. Jim and I had never been out of Nebraska, so we were amazed by the mountains and scenery in the west. We still talk about the train trip along the Columbia River into Portland. To save money, Mom fixed enough fried chicken for three days. It's a wonder we didn't have food poisoning.

Mom and I had plenty of time to talk about the court proceedings. I kept asking what I would have to say. As we got closer to Eugene I became more and more anxious and nervous about my meeting with Dad. I wouldn't know what to say to him because I still dreamed of a reconciliation. I hardly slept and didn't eat the night before, dreading the thought of going into the courtroom and testifying against him.

The three of us met Dad in the courthouse waiting room the morning of the trial. "Ed," Mom said. "This is your Dad." He didn't even look at me. Instead, he just stared at Mom and Jim. I just stood there and stared at him. My first impression upon seeing my father was, "My God! Who is this man? I don't know him. This man surely isn't my dad! My dad is tall and lean with dark hair!" I had to look up to him when I was a child but, measuring six feet at the time, I now had to look down at him. He was short with gray hair and a potbelly. This could hardly be the man I waited for all of those years. I'd met lots of men like him in his line of work and I didn't care to be around any of them. This was not the man I remembered as a kid and certainly less than the man I once loved and trusted.

"What the hell did you bring these two kids out here for?" he demanded. Mom didn't say a word. "This is between you and me," he said. "You had no business bringing them along. They don't need to get in the middle of this."

Mom began to cry. I stepped over, put my arm around her and said, "Mom, it's OK. I'm glad we're here." I became angry and wanted to strike out at this man for making my mother cry. If it were anybody else I could have done it, but I couldn't hit my father. I said nothing, but inside I was screaming at him for hurting Mom. Why didn't he just stop this foolishness and come home where he belonged. Neither of them knew what I was feeling. I was accustomed to keeping my feelings locked up for so long.

Our attorney, Frank Reid, took me aside and explained the procedure. "Ed, you will be called up to the judge to testify. Answer any questions he asks about your parents. He will question you about your dad's intentions to bring the family to live with him."

We were only a few minutes away from the hearing; I was scared to death and my stomach was in a mess. I was trembling by the time Mom and I were directed into the courtroom. Jim stayed in the reception room and the receptionist said she would watch him since it would only take a few minutes. The courtroom was cold and formal. I sat there waiting for the judge to arrive. Dad and his lawyer sat at a table across from us and several court workers were walking around preparing for the hearing. We were just another case on the docket to them but the upcoming event would change our family forever.

We were asked to stand as the judge entered the courtroom. The clerk of the court read the charge of desertion against Mr. Floyd E. Reinhardt to the court. The defense attorney sitting next to Dad was asked how his client would plead. "Innocent," was his reply. The attorney was asked to defend Dad's plea and began to talk. "Your Honor, Mr. Reinhardt has worked with Peter Kiewit Construction Company for many years. His work as a project superintendent is building roads for the northwest district of the Kiewit Company in Washington, Oregon and California. About five years ago, Mr. Reinhardt returned from building military installations in Alaska. At that time, and several times since, he has tried to persuade Mrs. Reinhardt to move out here from Nebraska so the family could be together. Your

Honor, Mr. Reinhardt was told she would not move the family away from Omaha and from her own family."

"Lies!" I thought. "All goddamn lies!" I couldn't believe what I was hearing! The son-of-a-bitch was telling the judge and the court all kinds of lies. I kept asking myself, "What kind of a man is Dad that he would just lie to the judge, to Mom and me and expect everyone to believe him?" For the first time in my life, I saw what a bastard he really was. I thought about having waited and waited and praying for him to come home. All of the humiliation and embarrassment I suffered, along with the fights and the bragging I did to uphold his honor, flashed through my mind as I sat there listening to his attorney. The attorney finally ended his remarks and sat down next to Dad.

Our attorney then stood up to address the judge. "Your Honor, I would like to tell you about Margaret Reinhardt, the defendant's wife. She has been married to Mr. Reinhardt for nearly thirty years. Together they have six children. For nearly ten years, Mr. Reinhardt has been working away from home. The first five years he was in Alaska. Prior to this, Mr. Reinhardt had various construction jobs around Nebraska and each time the family moved with him. Only once in those five years did Mr. Reinhardt come home from Alaska to be with his family. That was only to recover from a work-related injury. Mr. Reinhardt hasn't been home during the past five years either. Five years is a long time to be away from a wife, for any reason."

Dad's attorney objected to our attorney's reference to Dad not having any interest in being with his wife. However, the judge directed our attorney to proceed.

He talked about her efforts to educate us, the successes of her son, John, in the Navy, and her daughter, Rita, in the Marine Corps during the war. He told about my attending college at Omaha University and about how hard I studied and how well I was getting along. I hoped he hadn't done too much investigating or he would have met up with my last report card. The kind words said about my mother made me feel proud. My love poured out to her and I promised myself I would always look after her.

Then it was my turn. Mr. Reid asked the judge to accept me as a witness and the judge directed me to take the stand. I reached the stand and looked straight ahead at my mother. The judge recognized my fear and spoke to me in a soft, reassuring voice. He explained the procedures of his court and the actions about to take place between my mother and father.

As I listened to the judge's gentle voice, I began to cry. Quietly, I told the judge my story, about how I didn't want the divorce. The judge could sense my disapproval but knew neither of us could change my parents' minds; in a few minutes, a decision would be reached.

"Floyd Edward," he began. "Do you understand the charges against your father?"

"Yes, your Honor."

"Do you understand your father tried twice to divorce your mother and both times the court denied his request because he had no grounds to get the divorce. In other words, the courts found no reason to dissolve their marriage. There was no negligence on your mother's part for him to get the divorce."

"Yes sir, I understand."

"Do you believe your father deserted your mother and you kids?"

I could not speak and only looked at him and nodded. Tears were running down my face. The judge paused a moment as I wiped my eyes, then asked another question. "Floyd Edward, did your mother ever refuse to move the family to live with your dad?"

I felt awkward when he called me by my first name, Floyd, since I hadn't used that name since the fourth grade. Quietly, I told him, "Dad never asked Mom to move out west."

"Do you think your mom would have moved to be with your dad?"

"For years I looked forward to reading Dad's letters each month, hoping someday he would come home or take us to be with him just like he promised. After a while he stopped writing and just sent money. Two years ago he stopped sending money and Mom had to go to work. We moved six times before Dad left home because of work. We would have moved this time, too, but he didn't ask."

The judge paused for a moment, then, staring at me he said in a quiet voice, "Floyd Edward, you're a nice young man. Stay in school. That will be all. You may return to your place." I stepped away from the judge's bench and sat down next to our attorney.

Mr. Reid looked over at me and said with a smile, "You did fine."

Mom's kind smile made me feel better. It seemed like the world had just been lifted from my shoulders.

The rest of the proceeding was a formality for the court workers. Finally, the judge brought down the gavel with words which still ring in my ears: "Divorce granted."

Why Do We Have to Say Goodbye?

CHAPTER 8

*J*n her book *In The Heart of the World*, Mother Teresa says, "There is much suffering in the world—very much. Material suffering is suffering from hunger, suffering from homelessness, from all kinds of disease, but I still think the greatest suffering is to be lonely, feeling unloved, just having no one. I have come more and more to realize that it is being unwanted that is the worst disease that any human being can ever experience."

I hate saying goodbye to anyone. It seems so permanent. There is an empty feeling, a loneliness, and sometimes a feeling of despair saying goodbye to relatives—especially my children. I have to dig deep down to find peace and search for some joy to make me feel better. I have to find the pieces to rebuild a life I feel is lost during the separation. I avoid saying goodbye when I can and plan to be busy for a while after a departure.

After the proceedings, Dad took Jim and me to lunch and entertained us with stories about workers on his construction crew, building roads and the Oregon weather. I laughed and shared a few experiences from working on the farm and from college. My stomach was churning as I awaited what was just ahead. Dad drove us around Eugene and the University of Oregon campus. We walked around the administration offices and under the vine-covered trellis, a popular place for sweethearts to stroll between classes. I wished Donna were along as I thought about taking off her glasses and kissing her as we walked along the way.

We walked over to the football field. I would never have guessed someday I would walk under the same trellis and past the same buildings, when I had to decide to sign a paper stating, if my son died here, we would donate his organs to help others. Nor would I have guessed ten years after Eddie was injured here, our youngest son Matthew would play football for this same Oregon football team.

We arrived at the ice cream store around four o'clock to meet Mom and have a treat before saying our farewells. I tried to keep the conversation going because of the uneasiness I felt between my parents as they were about to end their relationship of nearly 30 years. I believed Dad would walk away feeling relieved, continuing on without feelings of remorse.

Mom would go away feeling sad and hurt and unloved by the man she loved since the day they met. Mom would not know or enjoy romantic love from another man for the rest of her life. She was a beautiful and kind woman whom many men wanted to marry, but none would ever win her affection. Dad did not recognize the treasure he had. He'd learn.

Three months after their divorce he remarried. One of the conditions of marriage was he would have a vasectomy before their wedding. It seemed to me she found it convenient to have a man around the house. He became the maintenance man for her motel, he did extensive remodeling to her house and he developed the 80 acres of land they put in her name. She died suddenly after 20 years of marriage and all of her property was willed to her son from her first marriage. Dad was left with nothing.

Mom would also go away from the divorce knowing she had the love and support of her six children. All of us loved her and each, in our own way, took care of her until she died in 1986.

Our conversation was lagging and I felt it was time to leave and say goodbye for the last time. I began to breathe quickly and deeply because I knew I must say goodbye without crying. I had to leave behind all my feelings for Dad there in Eugene that day because I believed he would never love or care for me again. My love for him had to stay there in the memory of the ice cream store, the courtroom, the hotel and even the train depot. Those memories could no longer be part of my life. Eugene was a good place to leave my love for Dad. It was an out-of-the-way city and I would probably never be back again.

It was cold and raining that late afternoon in February as we stood on the corner of Broadway and Pearl outside the ice cream store. We were friendly and all smiling, shaking hands and repeating our goodbyes and so longs. The traffic light had changed three times and it became obvious we had to turn and start walking across the street. My guts were on fire. Nothing was said about getting together for a visit or even a phone call. I realized this time with Dad was over. With a smile, I looked at him a final time, shook his hand and turned to leave. As I walked between Mom and Jim with my arms on their shoulders, my smile quickly changed to tears.

By the time we crossed the street, Mom and Jim were crying too. As we stepped up on the curb, I turned to look back. Dad was already gone. I wanted to be strong for them as we walked to the Eugene Hotel and fought back my own tears while I tried to console them.

I don't remember much about that night. Years later my younger brother said, "You headed straight for bed and didn't get up until just before we checked out of the hotel the next morning. You didn't say anything to either of us. You didn't even eat dinner or breakfast that morning. You were out of it." Of all the things that happened on that trip, this memory is one of the few Jim has carried with him. From the time I reached the bed until the next day somewhere north of San Francisco, I don't know what happened. It was like I had been in a coma.

The next night in the light of the full moon, the train reached Utah. I could see the mountains and desert as we traveled at high speed. It was dark inside of our train car. Jim was curled up across from me next to Mom and both of them were sleeping peacefully. I was pleased to see that. I knew I would always be there for them.

I stared out the window and considered what was ahead for me. Thinking about school and how hard I tried to study on this trip and the unfinished homework, made me discouraged about my education. I wondered, "Why the hell am I even going to school. I have no idea what I want to do with my life. I was not sure I could succeed at any job based on the constant failure I experienced with my schoolwork."

I thought about my friends in Sigma Phi Epsilon, a fraternity I had pledged earlier in the school year, and how out of place I felt attending pledge classes and parties in the homes of other pledges. Here was the dad in his expensive home, smoking his pipe and reading his newspaper while the mom was in the kitchen baking cookies. Everything seemed just fine with them.

Meanwhile, Mom was trying to scrape up enough money to pay the mortgage by renting out half the house to boarders. Feeling too uncomfortable trying to be part of their world, I ended my membership in the fraternity soon after I returned to school.

I thought about Donna and how lonely I felt being away from her. She was the only bright spot in my life then. As soon as she came into my mind, doubts followed. "What makes me think I'm stable enough to be married and raise a family? How could I learn to settle down and go to work every day for the rest of my life? What do I know about being a husband and father?" I was very much aware I had my father's blood. At nineteen, I too longed for the things the world had to offer but, on this night, I was lonely and just wanted to be close to Donna.

I thought about God and how I was taught to trust in Him to answer my prayers. I thought about all the masses I'd attended, asking God to bring Dad home, believing someday he would return. Mom had told me over and over Dad would come home someday, I saw her dreams shattered too. I felt foolish and angry about expecting anything to come from prayer and thought about how I wasted a lot of time asking for Dad to come home. Did I expect him to show up unannounced one morning and simply say, "I'm home?"

My relationship with God changed after the divorce in Eugene. I became less trusting and less dependent on God. I did all of the things I was taught as a Roman Catholic, but deep down inside I realized my life was mine to carve out the best I could. I decided I would be smarter than to depend on God or to believe He would answer my prayers. Eventually, my belief in God weakened so much I wouldn't need Him at all. I decided I wouldn't get close to anyone again and would always keep some distance from people so I wouldn't be hurt again.

If I wanted anything out of life, I would have to make it happen. If I wanted to go back to college or have a car or have any kind of a life, I had to make it happen. OK, if this is the way life is, I'll do it. In the future, Frank Sinatra's song would become mine. "I Did it My Way." This is how I would protect myself from ever getting hurt again. People would have to pass a lot of tests and jump through lots of hoops before trust even started to develop.

I thought about my dad and all the events of the day before. "Where is he and what is he doing right now?" I wondered. "Is he feeling any regret about the divorce or is he celebrating the end of a meaningless part of his life? Is he remembering the time spent with Jim and me and does he ever want to see us again?"

Obviously not, since he never asked about visiting rights or even asking us to visit him. I wondered why I felt so strange and indifferent toward him then. I didn't feel any great sorrow about what just happened in Eugene. I had no feelings of great loss or disappointment and I was relieved it was over. Last night my future looked so hopeless. In fact I started to feel some enthusiasm about getting home and getting started with my life again. By tomorrow night, I would be home. I could hardly wait to get back to Omaha. I was dying to see Donna and hold her glasses.

Commitments Don't Come Easy

After I returned from Oregon in February of 1952, I turned my attention away from Dad and thought more about plans for my future. I struggled through to the end of my first year in college and decided to go to work and not return to school in the fall. I felt I had too many problems in high school and college and with the emotional upheaval I'd been through with the divorce, I needed some time to pursue other interests. Besides, I was nearing draft age and decided just to wait and be drafted into the army.

The alimony and child support check sent to Mom from Dad through the Oregon social services was barely enough for Mom and my little brother. So by working, I could help out at home until I left for the service.

A terrible loss happened to a member of my extended family. My aunt Adelaide, mother's sister-in-law, died during childbirth, so Mom decided to help her brother and his seven kids by moving them in with us. The oldest was in the seventh grade. There were twelve of us at home then and we expected my uncle and his children to stay with us for a few years. Mom always looked out for others and seldom complained. Her example taught me about being generous and sharing with others. My uncle's children brought us a lot of joy and much laughter.

Occasionally I would see Donna. Each time we met, the wonderful feelings I had for her returned. As those feelings came back to me, I would begin to think about my fear of getting married. I struggled with doubts of my ability to support and raise a family. The freedom I was enjoying was more exciting and safer than getting married. After I entered the army, our relationship slowly ended.

The Korean War was still going on during the fall of 1952. Several of my buddies had volunteered that fall for the Nebraska Army National Guard and within six months, two were killed and one came home without a leg. I was a year younger than they were and wasn't drafted until July of 1953, five days before the fighting in Korea ended.

Before I was drafted, my contribution to the war was working with the American Red Cross. I worked in the blood-mobile unit and we collected blood throughout Nebraska and Iowa. The plasma was shipped directly to Korea. I especially liked this job because it offered lots of traveling. All of the mobile unit sites were staffed by volunteers who helped the nurses move donors through health checks to determine whether they were eligible to donate. One of the volunteers would eventually become my mother-in-law.

I thought my incessant need to travel and see the world would be satisfied in the Army since foreign travel seemed to be reserved for people with money. "See the world through a porthole or out the back of a two-and-a-half-ton truck" is what I heard from homecoming veterans. Either way, I would gladly serve my military duty if I could go overseas.

We started with sixteen weeks of basic training at Fort Leonard Wood, Missouri. My initial attitude was to be the biggest screw-off in the Army. After three weekends of kitchen duty, I realized this wasn't the way I wanted to spend my military obligation. I decided to listen to what the Army had to say. I finished the first eight weeks of training and then moved on to become a squad leader for the second half. Without the influence of teachers and family I learned more about myself and how I functioned with others. I learned I could do as well as any other soldier. Finally, I felt the acceptance I had been seeking from my superiors in the army.

After graduating from basic training, I held my breath as I waited for my assignment. There were two assignments: Korea or Germany. We had no choice in the matter. The decision was made in typical Army fashion. The fateful decision of where we would spend the next two years was determined by whether we were odd or even numbered as we stood in formation. One to Korea, one to Germany, one to Korea, one to Germany, then one to Alaska. . . then the selection process repeated itself. I let out an excited yell when I learned I was going to Germany.

Two days later I arrived home on leave for ten days before going overseas. While I was graduating from training, my mother had fallen and broken her arm and was in the hospital, but no one had sent word to me about her accident. My old boss at the American Red Cross told me I could easily obtain a hardship discharge to stay home with Mom and my brother Jim.

Instantly, I felt anger toward my father because I knew he should be the one at home caring for our family.

"When will I have the freedom to live my own life?" I wondered. "Why do I always have to get my family mixed up with the things I want to do?" Then I felt guilty about my selfishness. I thought, "If Dad had died when I was young, at least I would have a clearer understanding of my family responsibilities. I would do what I had to do." But with him alive, I just felt neglected by him. My alternating love-hate feelings for him kept me in constant turmoil. My anger would build until I felt I would like to kill him if I could just get my hands around his neck.

My four older siblings were very good about looking after Mom, so I decided she could get along without me. Mom encouraged me not to apply for a hardship discharge, but to go to Germany—to travel and to see as much of Europe as I could. She even said if I needed money to travel, she would help out. I thanked her for her blessing and promised her I wouldn't let her down. I also promised I would go to Ireland and learn about her Irish heritage. Her encouragement taught me not to be satisfied with what life gave me, but rather to look for the good which could happen through my own initiative and hard work. Her encouragement to forgive and respect my dad and to pray for him to come home, became such a part of me that it would become my life goal to make it happen.

Europe was more than I ever expected. I traveled to twelve countries and some of the largest cities. The Army gave me security, which I grew to appreciate. I liked the order and daily routine it provided with exceptionally clean living conditions and good meals served three times a day. I gained thirty pounds during the first three months in the army and lost the same amount three months after my discharge. The army gave me a chance to succeed and excel as a company supply clerk. We worked hard in our outfit. I earned a letter of recommendation from my commanding officer to use as a reference for future employment and also received a good behavior medal. I had come a long way since fifth grade with Sister Mary Damian!

In Germany, I wrote to Donna, saying nothing about a commitment. In her last letter she talked about the relationship she had with a guy in the Navy and about how he wanted to marry her. He asked her to stop writing to me and she needed to know if there was anything meaningful left between us. In my last letter, I tried to explain my uncertainty about the future and how concerned I was about my ability to be a good husband and provider. I was afraid to tell her how much I loved her and wanted her to marry me. I explained how I had some unfinished business at home which kept me from making any long-range plans. I didn't ask her to wait. Donna was married three weeks before I got back from Europe and for several years I believed I had made a mistake. My inability to commit had come back to haunt me—and it wouldn't be the last time.

During the early '50s in Germany there was little association between the GIs and girls living at home with their families. If they weren't working the streets as prostitutes, they were at home being watched over by parents who kept their daughters away from the soldiers who roamed the streets of Munich. Europe was filled with more than a million combat troops exercising their midnight and weekend passes and trying to drink all the

German beer they could hold, while sitting alongside of a German fraulein, who for 100 marks—about 25 dollars—would take them home for the night.

The German civilian in charge of all the German workers in our outfit was named Schroeder. He had been a cook in the German Army during World War II and liked me because I was of German descent on my father's side. I was also the company supply clerk and he saw to it I was well fed. I reciprocated with the supplies he needed each month to pass mess hall inspections.

It was unusual for a GI to be invited into a German home because there was still resentment toward the Americans. Nevertheless, Schroeder and I became friends and he sometimes invited me to his home for dinner on Sundays or holidays. Germans had a lot of holidays. I enjoyed being with his family and especially enjoyed meeting his daughter Uschie. Uschie was blonde with sparkling blue eyes and her skin was soft and smooth. She reminded me of Donna. We were both 21.

Uschie liked to listen to me tell about America. I felt proud of my many experiences growing up, the places I had traveled throughout the United States and the countries I had visited in Europe. She made me feel good about myself and I knew she liked me because she was always anxious for us to be together. I told the Schroeders only enough about my family to satisfy their curiosity. I bragged a lot about my mother and explained how much her Irish heritage was so much like the German people of Bavaria. Most of our time together was spent at home with the family and never out of Schroeder's view. He liked me a lot but I'm not sure he trusted me alone with Uschie. Occasionally, we would go out to a German restaurant or to church together as a family, never alone.

A normal custom on holidays was to share a friendly greeting, so New Year's Eve of 1955, Schroeder invited his friends and relatives in for a party. At midnight I made my rounds greeting the family and was finally allowed, under the guise of the holiday, to kiss Uschie. Uschie didn't wear glasses. I thought then Uschie could be the girl I wanted to marry. All I wanted was the assurance our life together would be happy and I could be a good husband and father. I knew nothing in life was for certain, but the possibility I would follow in my father's footsteps haunted me. The doubts in my mind seemed to never go away.

My last Sunday afternoon and evening in Germany was spent with Uschie and her family. During the days before we said goodbye, I struggled with the idea of getting married and bringing her back to America.

The evening was quiet and when it was time to leave, her family joined me at the door. I hugged her mother and her sister and shook hands with her brothers and Schroeder. It was April, four months since our New Year's Eve kiss. With her dad's silent approval and tears in our eyes, I put my arms around her and kissed her the second and last time. I thought I was making a mistake by not bringing her home. For a second time, I was unable to make a commitment.

My homecoming from Germany was exciting. When we docked in New York Harbor, the band played and families cheered as 2500 men disembarked from the ship. At home, it was less ceremonious. I arrived home one day in early summer and found Mom and Jim were both out of town. My grandmother had suffered a stroke and Mom was in O'Neill with her. Mom had quit her job a few months earlier to take care of her mother. I found unpaid house payments and utility bills and could see the house needed repairs and painting. Independent and feeling successful about my military service, I was frustrated and angry again at the situation in which I found myself. The money I had saved for college would be needed to pay the mortgage and for the cost of repairs. "What am I supposed to do, just walk away from Mom and Jim?" I wondered. I felt like leaving them and starting out on my own, but was immediately overwhelmed with guilt. I became angry at my dad all over again.

I took the night train to O'Neill and by morning was at my grandmother's side. She hadn't recognized any of the family for several weeks and they didn't expect her to know me. Mom and I entered her room and Mom explained to her Tubby had just come home from Germany. I was saddened to see my grandmother like this, but I was determined to tell her I had been to Ireland. I hardly said the words when she looked right at me and said, "Oh, Tubby! You look just like your dad!" She looked at me for another moment, then turned away. I cried a long time that morning, especially because I wasn't able to tell her more about Ireland. That was the last time she would recognize any of us. She died a few months later.

I re-entered school at the University of Omaha in 1955. This was a school which referred to itself as the University of Omaha Mavericks. I mused, "I no longer *think* I'm a maverick, I *am* one." I began to settle down to my studies and occasionally thought about my dad.

It had been nearly five years since Dad's last letter with alimony and child support payments. We didn't know where he was. I wondered if he was even alive and started asking about how to find people who had dropped out of sight. My law professor explained how easy it was to drop from sight and how hard it would be to go to court for back child support when we lived two thousand miles away from Dad.

"States try to protect their citizens from harassment if the missing persons are law-abiding citizens and good taxpayers," he said. "About the only way to bring a court action would be to move to that state and spend the time needed to file and be there for the hearings. Eventually there would be a trial but all of the legal work could take up to a year." My plans to find my dad were shelved again as I began to think about my future after school and the possibility of meeting the right girl.

At twenty-five, I was a confirmed bachelor by most standards. I was still uncertain about my career and disappointed about not graduating with my class, since I had to repeat the classes I had failed my freshman year.

One weekend my friend Gary Grummond suggested I go on a blind date with him and his wife. I would typically disregard such suggestions back then because I felt too uncomfortable. Besides, getting dates wasn't the problem. The problem was the commitment. This weekend, however, I was feeling depressed over my missed graduation and unknown future. I thought, "What the hell, why not!"

The date was January 25, 1959. We were having a severe cold spell in Omaha and, earlier that Sunday afternoon, I nearly lost a yard stick measuring the depth of the snow in our front yard. The temperature was well below zero.

My sister Bunny and her husband Frank stopped over for dinner and Bunny casually asked, "Hi Ed, What's going on?"

"Aw, not much, Bun. I just finished finals on Friday and to-night I have a blind date. You know me, I usually turn down those offers, but this one feels different. I can't understand why I'm kind of excited about going out, even in this weather."

However, when I reached the front steps of my date's apart-ment, I developed cold feet and turned to leave. Gary stepped in front of me, blocking the steps. I quickly turned back toward the door and said to Gary, "What's her name?" The door opened before he could answer and there stood this girl. "WOW! Surely, no girl so beautiful would need to rely on a blind date," I thought. "Maybe we are on the wrong porch." I hoped we weren't. We were invited inside and introduced to each other. Her name was Pat.

We went to a movie and stopped for something to eat after-wards. I couldn't take my eyes off her. She was tall, with long dark hair, brown eyes and a perpetual smile extending from ear to ear. I had seldom dated many tall girls because, like many guys, I felt threatened by their size. Her height was of little con-cern to me then. I became totally infatuated by her outward appearance and was anxious to get a glimpse of the person in-side. Her voice was low. She spoke softly and expressed her thoughts slowly, compelling me to give her every bit of my at-tention. I became quiet just so I could hear her voice. She seemed kind and thoughtful when describing her work as a nurse at the hospital. It made me think about how much she reminded me of my mother.

Later on, I learned she was impressed I wore a suit and vest, was an usher in our church and had been to Europe. She hadn't traveled much out of Nebraska and was impressed when I told her about my adventures as a soldier in Germany. She even liked the idea of my smoking a pipe.

That evening, and the days to follow, were exhilarating for me. I couldn't wait until the next time we would be together. I invited her to sporting and musical events at the college and we began attending church together. I wanted to be with her all the time and seldom thought about the insecurities I had about being a good husband and father. My self-confidence grew and I finally developed a sense of what I wanted to do. I was determined to have Pat for my wife.

Pat was the oldest of six children, a graduate nurse and the apple of her parents' eyes. She was a daddy's girl and he kept both eyes on her most of the time. Her dad ruled the family and when he wanted something done everybody jumped. He was a good husband and father but, as usual, I felt intimidated by him as an authority figure.

During one of our visits to her parents' farm, I hoped to impress her father with how much I, a city boy, knew about farm work. They seemed surprised to see me milk a cow. I explained how I had spent several summers on my grandparents' farm working in the hayfields with the horses. I asked him if he had any work I could do for him.

His was a crop farm with cattle and hogs, and haying wasn't part of the operation. He had lots of equipment but no horses, and nobody else was allowed to operate the tractors. My only experience with machinery had been heavy road equipment, so it seemed there was little chance I could impress him.

Then I remembered my trip to the hen house with Pat earlier that morning. We had gone to gather eggs and I had tried to kiss her. Gagging from the odor, we went out and kissed behind the barn. Seeing the hens scratching in 12 inches of manure gave me an idea.

Without thinking I blurted out, "How about letting me clean your chicken coop." I remembered back to the time I cleaned spittoons in my uncle's tavern and thought, "If I could clean spittoons, I could make this coop sparkle." It also might be the price I had to pay to marry his daughter. A slight smile came over his face as if he were pleased at my initiative. He was probably overjoyed to find a sucker who would clean up the chicken poop! He graciously offered to let me use the manure spreader to re-locate the stuff onto the cornfields. Best of all, I was allowed to use the tractor. This was a big concession for a farmer, allowing a city boy to operate equipment, and word spread fast around the family.

By Saturday afternoon, three days and five loads later, the hens were allowed back in their castle and I headed for a long shower. It seemed like weeks before the dust was out of my lungs and I could breathe again.

Sunday would be our last day on the farm and after dinner we would drive back to Omaha. All morning I tried to be alone with her parents so I could ask them for their daughter's hand in marriage. The kids had left us talking at the kitchen table and I blurted out the question. I tried to explain how much I loved their daughter and how much I wanted to marry her. They recognized my shyness and my sincerity and they both agreed. I breathed a sigh of relief after their approval and gave Pat a kiss.

Search for Dad

With the prospect of getting married the following year, I was uneasy about the unfinished business I had at home. Mom had been working and was financially independent and Jim was entering college. I realized it was no longer my responsibility to stay home with them and Mom assured me I was free to go on with my own life. She gave her blessing when we announced our engagement, but I was still determined to find Dad. If he wouldn't come home, then at least he would be made accountable for the money he owed the family. Eight years of back child support and alimony would be a substantial amount of money for Mom. Since I was finishing school, I decided to try to find him and get this settled prior to finding permanent work and being married.

I believed he was still working for Peter Kiewit and, since we nearly lived in the shadow of company headquarters in Omaha, I began my search with them. I was anxious as I entered their new modern facilities and felt threatened by the professional response from the receptionist. Timidly, I introduced myself as a son of one of their employees who worked in Oregon and explained how I had lost contact with my dad and wanted to know where he was working. That got me past the receptionist and to the personnel director.

Unfortunately, she was unsympathetic to my plight. She stated it was company policy not to give out any information about employees without the employee's permission. I told her I understood the policy but this was my dad, and I needed to locate him. I asked her to please tell me if he was still employed with Kiewit. Her tight smile and crossed arms told me our conversation was over.

My determination to keep looking grew. I would have to go to Oregon with few leads but I would not dismiss the whole matter. My compulsion to find my dad was not to be denied if I were ever to start a life of my own.

I did not discuss my quest with my family and why I was going to such effort because no one ever talked about Dad nor seemed to care if he ever came home. Some of my siblings were shocked when I announced I was leaving for Oregon to look for Dad. I confided in Pat and she encouraged me to follow my plan to search for him.

We had a few old letters which listed job locations where he had worked and I thought I would start tracking him down with those leads. His last address was in a place called McCredie Springs, Oregon, just outside Eugene. In earlier letters, he mentioned a place in eastern Oregon, called the Dexter Lake Club. Dad wasn't much for sports or social clubs, so this was unusual, but it was still a lead and I would search for him there as well. I had the address of Frank Reid, Mom's divorce attorney, and hoped he could help my search for Dad.

It was early August of 1960 when I started out on my quest. My emotions, thinking I might actually find Dad, ranged from feeling ridiculous to fearing that I might meet up with him.

Mom was the only one in the family who encouraged my efforts. She knew all along of my need to have a relationship with him. She admired my efforts and bravery in going alone. Even though I couldn't identify what I needed from finding Dad, she never denied my feelings. Her confidence moved me forward.

My first new car had aged into an eight-year-old car, which would require a whole case of motor oil for a trip like this. Once the oil was loaded, I set off for Oregon alone. I started the 1600 mile drive to Eugene by heading west on U.S. Highway 30, which took me across Nebraska, Wyoming and up into Idaho; then along Highway 20, over McKenzie Pass on 242 and 126, into Eugene. I stopped in Burley, Idaho, to visit my cousin, Pat Hynes, but learned from his neighbors he had just moved to Nevada to work on the railroad. It was a disappointment and, already, the trip wasn't starting off like I planned. The next afternoon I reached the Dexter Lake Club, just inside the Oregon border. I was surprised Dad would have any connection with a restaurant or boat rental business, and there seemed to be few roads to build around the small resort area.

It was a quiet Wednesday afternoon when I arrived. The lake was about the size of ten football fields and I could see a boat pulling a skier on the far end, but it was mostly used for sailing. "How do you find someone in a place like this?" I thought. "Go door to door?" For starters, all I could see was a grocery store, a gas station and, of course, a couple of bars near the water. The Dexter Lake Club, a bar, sat near the water and had the only activity in town.

I had seen a lot of movies where the stranger in town walked in and started a conversation with the bartender, so I thought that it must be the way it was done. I walked through the lobby and found the bar. I ordered a beer and began talking to the bartender. I quietly asked him, "Have you ever heard of a guy named Reinhardt? Floyd Reinhardt?"

His response was nothing like the movies. "Nah! I don't know many people around here. I just moved over from the coast. I close the bar and clean up around here after sundown. Ain't much going on when the lake closes in the afternoon. The owners just left for the day. They work 'til after lunch, then come back here in the morning. You might stay over 'til morning and talk with the owners. They might know him. There's a motel just down the road." After another beer and a couple of cigarettes, I wished him well and headed for Eugene so I could get there before dark. Seven years later I learned more about the Dexter Lake Club. I should have listened to the bartender.

As I traveled farther into Oregon I stopped at several construction sites to ask workers if they'd ever heard of my dad. Finally, a traffic flagman thought he remembered a guy named Reinhardt. "Didn't he work for Kiewit?" he asked. "I worked on a job over around Crescent City, in California, and might have worked for him. The guy I knew was a tough son-of-a-bitch, and you had better wanna work if you were working for him. We knew to never come to work drunk or he'd run us off the job. He didn't take any crap from anyone." I was sure this guy had the right man, and it sounded as if Dad hadn't lost his touch. I often told myself it was probably better for me in some ways he was gone from home because I would have driven him crazy, or he would have killed me because of my orneriness.

Eugene hadn't changed much in eight years. The large "EUGENE HOTEL" sign still stood as a landmark and the ice cream store still sold the best ice cream in town. I hadn't spoken to anyone I knew for four days and visiting those familiar places and the street corner where I said goodbye to Dad only served to increase my loneliness. I hadn't thought much about what I'd say if I met up with Dad. I wished I wouldn't have to face him alone. It was easy for me to think about facing him when I was back in Nebraska, 1700 miles away, but I was frightened to think about our meeting here in his own back yard.

I had talked with the parents of a high school buddy back in Omaha and was told their son lived in Eugene and worked in a paint store. I was anxious to connect with someone, so the next morning I started looking for the store and my friend, Don Deiley. When I got to the paint store, I was told he had quit and left Eugene about a week earlier. I was beginning to feel very much alone in my quest for Dad. Another door had been closed.

After grabbing some lunch, I found Frank Reid's office. Hoping to have contact with somebody, I entered the office and asked the receptionist for Mr. Reid.

"Mr. Reid is out of the city on vacation for two weeks and won't return until mid- September," the receptionist told me. She left no doubt I wasn't going to find, or talk to, Mr. Reid. "May I help you with something?" she asked.

"I'm looking for my dad," I mumbled.

"Excuse me?" she asked.

"Mr. Reid helped us eight years ago during my parents' divorce and I'm looking for my dad."

"Well, we wouldn't have any records of that. You might try the city directory at the library," she said before lowering her head. The conversation was over and the door closed.

I spent the next morning searching at the library. I went back through the city directories. Their phone books covered only Eugene and towns within a radius of fifty miles. Communications in 1960 were nothing like they are today. To locate anyone through telephone information you had to know the name of the town, and it wasn't practical to choose all the towns in Oregon. I would not be discouraged and started researching my final lead—the last address on his letters. McCredie Springs, I discovered, was located a few miles outside of Eugene. I asked several people for directions and was told to drive an exact distance on a certain road until I came to an old road sign which read "McCredie Springs." I didn't see anything resembling a motel, but did come upon a burned-out shell of a long, L-shaped building which appeared to have twelve sets of walls and a foundation. Obviously, fire had destroyed the place at least five years before, as the heavy underbrush and trees were taking over the area. Nothing here could tell me anything about Dad's whereabouts.

Fruitlessly, I spent another few days talking to contractors at construction companies. Most were too busy and not forthcoming. I was told many of their road workers were paid by the day and records were seldom kept for part-time employees. My car had been stalling out, so after spending most of my remaining expense money on repairs, I decided to leave for home the following day. "Maybe it's just not supposed to be. Too many things just didn't happen during the trip," I thought. As far as I was concerned, my search was finished and the idea of finding him would have to wait for another time. With wedding plans ahead of me, I would be too busy to make further attempts to track him down for a reconciliation. I was never quite sure what I wanted from him anyway. All I knew was, somewhere deep inside of me, there was a flicker of yearning to regain our relationship. There was something I needed so badly from Dad, I just couldn't let go of him.

Reunited

Pat and I set our wedding date for July 8, 1961, one year after my failed trip to Oregon to search for Dad. We were married on her birthday. We had a beautiful church wedding and spent our honeymoon camping in the Black Hills of South Dakota. I was always sorry I didn't have a chance to reunite with Dad before I was married. (I believed I would have gained some insight into myself which would help me understand my fear of getting married.) It still seemed like I couldn't separate myself from the father-child relationship I had with my dad. Meeting him could help me see myself as an adult and I could move on with my life. Therefore, the doubt and the uncertainty of maintaining a lasting marriage was always in my mind. After our wedding, I put my thoughts about Dad in a distant corner.

I took a job selling business products with Control Data Corporation and moved our little family to Sioux City, Iowa. Sales was challenging and rewarding. I thrived on competing for awards and reaching quotas. I received the 100 percent Club membership each year and was rewarded with fabulous vacation award trips around the United States and Mexico. My motivator, money, served me well as an incentive to work harder to provide for my family. Promotions into major accounts took us to Columbia, Missouri, and finally to Denver as a district sales manager. Eventually, We started our own business selling computer supplies and printed business forms and when the kids were ready for college, so was the money. It also gave me the control and independence I needed.

Our first two children, John and Rosemarie were born in Omaha, Edward and Tom were born in Sioux City, Paul in Missouri and Matthew waited until we moved to Denver. We were seldom separated as a family.

Pat has always been a fantastic mother for our children. However, her decision to stay home after we were married was difficult for me to accept. I felt having two incomes would help us get started. (Our married friends were both working and living in nicer apartments than we were and they were driving better cars.) Her decision not to pursue her profession as a registered nurse became a gift to the children and helped them develop into healthy, well-adjusted people. Patiently, she insisted on nursing the babies, providing good nutrition and developing their intellects with frequent trips to the library. There was also quiet time.

I appreciated her demand for a stable routine for the kids. I was poor at establishing much order around our home. Sometimes I must have seemed like one of the kids to Pat. Once a neighbor kid asked Pat if Mr. Reinhardt could come out and play.

One day I stopped home for lunch and we began talking about all the work and constant demands of the kids. I could sense Pat's frustration to the point of panic so I tried to encourage her by explaining just how short our time would be with the kids. I tried to visualize them going off to college and moving away from the family. She sighed and said, "I don't know how you can see them in college when I can hardly see them past lunchtime."

I had taken little time during those years to think about Dad. I believed he was still working on road construction on the West Coast. Even if he were still alive, I had no idea where he lived or anything about his personal life. I decided we both had our own lives to live and I accepted the idea he wanted nothing to do with me as his son. Occasionally I felt the anger rise when I was reminded of the financial hardships my mother endured without him. As I watched the years go by, it was easy to blame him for his treatment of Mom and her loneliness. I resented his arrogance in disregarding the support payments directed by the Oregon courts. I blamed the courts for their neglect in not enforcing the alimony laws.

Nevertheless, curiosity began to haunt me concerning his whereabouts and his activities. Once again I began to wonder if I could possibly find him and have a relationship. One day in the fall of 1965, I was standing in line to register our car when the idea struck me to contact the auto licensing departments of several West Coast states. Late that evening I had six letters ready asking them for his current address. I explained how I had lost contact with him while in the military service in Europe. As I waited each day for a return letter, my anxiety heightened about the possibility of finding him.

Finally, after about a month, the letters started coming back— California, Washington, Montana, Idaho and Colorado— all reporting they had no listing for a Floyd Earl Reinhardt. During the next two weeks, I was miserable. I was mad at myself for building up hope of ever having a relationship with him. When I was feeling my lowest and ready to give up, the letter arrived from Oregon. I tore it open. All of the information I needed was right there in black and white: his address, town, even the make, model and year of his automobile. He drove a 1964 Caterpillar yellow Ford pickup. The bottom of the letter listed the co-owner, his wife, Vivian.

I had always suspected he had married a second time, but not knowing for sure gave me some hope someday he would come home. The sickening feeling stayed with me for several days and grew worse when I decided I should tell Mom.

By then, 13 years of unpaid alimony and child support had built up to several thousand dollars still owed to Mom. After telling her I had found Dad, I said, "Let's go after him, Mom. Dad isn't going to get away with neglecting his family!" We decided initiating an alimony and child support court action in Oregon, a long distance from Omaha, would be fruitless. We therefore planned for Mom to move to Oregon. She would start the court procedures right in his own backyard. Within a month, Mom was packed and ready to move to Grants Pass, Oregon, where Dad had been living for several years. Just as we had expected, the filing and response dates, court hearings and the final judgement in Mom's favor, lasted a year and a half. She received $3,500 in cash and a judgment against him for $40,000. Dad claimed few assets listed in his name. Their home had a market value of more than a million and a half dollars. Unfortunately, the property was in his wife's name. More important to me than the financial arrangements were Mom and Dad's cordial meetings after each court hearing when they had lunch together. I wanted to believe they loved each other, despite what they did with their lives. Anyway, I know Mom always loved Dad.

I learned later, those times were among Mom's happiest days. She lived in a hotel apartment in downtown Grants Pass and attended Mass every morning at a nearby church. With Mom's outgoing personality and friendly spirit, it didn't take long for her to make friends. She became active in church projects and had lots of news to write home about. She loved Oregon and mentioned she should have been more assertive and followed Dad out west.

Mom and I made plans deciding, after the legal work was completed, I would drive to Oregon with my family and bring her home. Every day for two weeks I picked up the telephone to call Dad and, each time, I walked away frightened he might reject me. After church one Sunday, I gathered my courage and went straight to the phone and called. Barely able to breath, I was able to tell him my plans. He seemed excited about our visit. We talked in a friendly way but without any mention of Mom or the court proceedings. I didn't want him to know before our visit, I had been behind the court confrontation.

After the call, I felt numb and couldn't explain anything we had said to Pat. I went to our bedroom and stood there and cried until the tears were flowing down my face. I was thankful for the time by myself to think about the loneliness I felt without him, and I was joyful about our upcoming visit. Pat was happy I had made the call and looked forward to meeting her father-in-law for the first time.

We had one month to prepare. This reunion meant scraping up enough money and getting our equipment ready to camp out most of the time. I decided to cash in an old insurance policy. My equity was just enough for us to make the 1,700 mile-trip. We had an old Rambler station wagon with room for the three children. All our supplies were packed in a canvas bag tied to the roof. Our plan was to travel about 500 hundred miles each day and arrive in four days.

My meeting with Dad was approaching and all I could think of was our encounter. What would he say? What would I say? Would he dare talk about why he left home? Would I be honest with myself and not back down from his remarks? As we began the final leg into Grants Pass, I became unusually quiet. The kids were napping in the back while Pat was reading a book. I began to sniffle and Pat asked if I was getting a cold. "I don't think so," I answered, and after that response, I couldn't say any more. I kept telling myself I needed to be strong but the tears began to well up in my eyes until I could barely see the road. I had to pull over before we reached town. I began sobbing.

Pat was stunned by my behavior. She had experienced my crying only a few times before. I felt sick to my stomach as I realized I was about to meet Dad face to face. I believed I could no longer think of myself as a child and we would face each other as two men. I was afraid I wouldn't be strong enough to confront him about his deserting the family if the matter came up but I couldn't back down from anything. I had to be ready to face him and let him see what kind of man I had become. I was scared I would fail myself.

After arriving in Grants Pass, we went to the hotel to get Mom and then to the city park to let the kids have some time on the playground. I told her I had called Dad before leaving Iowa to tell him about our visit. She was pleased I was making the effort to talk to him and there was the possibility of starting a relationship. Again, her encouragement gave me the strength I needed to approach him.

The next afternoon Pat and I loaded up the kids and drove the eight miles out to his place off Murphy Road. Seeing his ranch home from the road brought back the memory of the ranch he had promised me. Dad's place was a large, two-story home on sixty acres of land on the side of a mountain. Two 60-foot pine trees stood on either side of the front yard. The place overlooked the Applegate River Valley, with a view that stretched for miles. Upon entering the drive, I felt envious we weren't able to share this place together.

It was unbearably quiet as I stood waiting for someone to answer the door. I waited and stared back at Pat in the car. At that moment, as I rang the bell once more, I wanted to be any place in the world except there. I was almost ready to leave when I heard someone behind the door rattling the chain lock. My heart went right up to my throat. The door opened and there stood my dad, even shorter and fatter than the last time I had seen him. The smile on his face was as wide as the double doors. "Well, I'll be damned! How are ya?" he said. "Come on in!" I passed on his offer of a handshake and gave him a big hug.

I was speechless, but managed to say weakly, "Hi, Dad, I'm your son Ed!" I was confused about what to do. For a moment I thought about Pat and the kids in the car and wanted them to be at my side. I hesitated about going in. I stumbled through my next sentence by saying, "Yeah, just a minute. I want to get Pat and the kids."

"Sure, hell yes! Let's bring 'em all in. I want 'em all in here!" he said.

I smiled at Pat as I went back to carry in Rosemarie and Edward who had fallen asleep. We moved through the house toward the kitchen where his wife Vivian offered us dessert and coffee and cookies for the kids. The kids were on their best behavior. I was proud of Pat and proud of the fact our kids would be the first of the grandchildren to meet their grandfather.

After cake and coffee, Dad invited us on a tour of his place. He walked out to the garden to see the potato patch with a motorized scarecrow used to keep out deer. He turned on the motor to entertain the kids and of course they didn't want him to shut it off. We looked over the six cattle he kept to keep down the grass.

We walked up the mountainside where he had rigged up a pipe to bring water down from the springs for the pond and irrigation system. Dad's cleverness would have taken him much farther in life if he'd had more formal education. Finally, I got to sit in his pickup. "Here is my buddy who helped me find my Dad," I thought.

The evening was perfectly quiet and peaceful. We spent the time talking about every relative we knew. I listened to stories about building roads on the West Coast, the Cascade Mountains and the Oregon weather.

I kept telling myself it was too soon to discuss what I needed to say. I promised myself someday we would talk about the years of silence. The small talk we engaged in throughout the evening did not resolve the questions so deeply embedded in my soul, but this was not the time. Not yet.

During our visit, I learned some things about his wife, Vivian. She operated a motel in Grants Pass, with her sister Judy, and she had one son from another marriage. Someday I would have to ask her about the motel business. She was surprised to see we had three children under four years old, and brashly said to Pat, "I hope you aren't planning to have any more children." We didn't have the nerve to tell her another Reinhardt was tucked away under Pat's blouse!

We made plans to get together the next day. I invited Dad to our motel to see my brother John Earl, John's wife Beth, and their two daughters. They, too, planned to meet Mom after the trial for our trip back home. Dad and John had parted ways 20 years before when John walked away from Dad on a job site. They met in front of the motel and right away the barriers began to fall. My hope was each member of the family would make the effort to meet and reconcile with Dad so we could become a complete family again.

We spent the following day at the ocean and had our fare-well dinner with my parents sitting together. It seemed awkward sitting across from the two of them as though nothing had ever happened. I would long remember the satisfaction of that experience and I felt it was worth all the effort it took to make it happen.

The following day was Monday and time to say goodbye and start back to Iowa. Dad met us before work at the motel in his 1964 yellow Ford pickup. I liked that pickup from the beginning and never imagined someday it would be mine, parked in my garage as it is to this day. Being left-handed like my dad, I continue wearing the paint off the steering wheel in the same places as Dad.

Mom was riding home with John and his family and I wanted to talk to her before they left. I stepped into her motel room and told her how happy I felt seeing Dad again. I tried to explain I had no hope Dad might come home someday, since he seemed relatively happy with Vivian and his work. Again, as if Mom could read the future, she assured me someday he would come home. I believed her and promised myself I would never lose hope. I would take advantage of every opportunity to make her prediction come true. As usual, Mom asked me if I had enough money to get back to Iowa. "Here's $20. You might have car trouble." As we left Grants Pass and headed east, I basked in the good feelings of having a father, one I could call or visit any time I wanted.

Waiting for Our Showdown

Six years had passed since we said "goodbye" outside the motel room in Grants Pass. I called him on holidays and on his birthday each year. It was a few years before I was able to recognize what it meant to me to have a father. Each year I would sweat out the task of finding just the right card to express my feelings. I certainly couldn't tell him "Thanks for being there when I needed you most." Or anything like the card I received recently from my daughter Rosemarie, which read "Thanks, Dad. For high standards. Gentle strength. Loving guidance. Strong support. Positive influence. Understanding soul. My biggest fan. A special bond. A true friend. An outstanding example. Challenging me. Teaching me. Raising me. Investing in my future. Asking challenging questions. Helping me find answers. Wise advice. Exceptional insights. Honest answers. Believing in me. Standing by me. Sharing your memories. BEING THERE."

I don't believe I deserve this much credit, but my daughter knows I love her and this card is her way of showing she returns my love. My cards to Dad would read, "Happy Father's Day. I hope your day is filled with sunshine." Until I could experience some deep sense of love from him, I wasn't able to bring myself to share my feelings with him. My expressions of love for him would have to wait. Those considerations seemed selfish and small in the light of our growing relationship, but my feelings of rejection and anger were so profound, I couldn't express more love for him than I actually had. I also hoped he would call me sometime during those years but I realized it was my idea to start this relationship and he wasn't about to take the risk of getting rejected by me. We had a lot of ground to cover before I could fully and freely express all the love I had for him. I knew I would have to go through the agony of getting to the bottom of the anger I had carried with me for nearly a lifetime. Someday we would have our showdown.

Meanwhile, I continued building a successful sales career in printed business forms and the computer supplies industry. I let it be known I wanted to get into sales management. Working on the road, away from an office for nearly ten years, I believed I was ready for more responsibility. With a growing family, I needed more money and didn't hesitate to accept a transfer to Columbia, Missouri, to maintain an established territory and develop larger accounts. After working for three years in the Columbia, Missouri territory, my boss, Dick Fieger, was anxious for me to move up but was smart enough to give me the training I needed to succeed. I appreciated his foresight and we became good friends.

Openings for managers in Omaha and Lincoln were available and I would call Dick and ask, "Now, boss, now?"

"You're not ready yet," he would reply. Waiting was nothing new to me. It wasn't long before Rich Sheridan, the West Coast regional manager, called to ask if I was interested in a job in Denver, Colorado, as district manager. "My God! YES!" I answered. We planned to meet in Houston a few days later for the job interview and, after one hour of talking about my goals, he said, "Go home and start packing, You're going to Denver." People have said things to me over the years which have made some impact on my life, but his parting words are among those jewels which have always stayed with me. He said, "Good luck, Ed. You're a diamond in the rough." Those few words confirmed my deep belief—I have what it takes.

While heading home I had a layover in Dallas and was anxious to tell Pat the news. I explained how Denver was part of the West Coast region and our quarterly sales meetings would be held near San Francisco. I continued on about living in Colorado and near the mountains when it dawned on me how close I would be to Grants Pass on my trips to San Francisco. I blurted out, "Pat, I can go up and visit Dad after our sales meetings!" She was excited for me and happy we would also be closer to her family in Nebraska. Two months later, in June 1972, with Pat and five children, we landed in our home in Littleton, Colorado. The next day I made my first visit to my new office.

Adjusting to an office routine and trying to accomplish work through others was new and frustrating for me during the first few months. The interruptions and demands of managing the salesmen seemed more challenging than managing my children. My new office was located in a divisional office of Control Data Corporation. There were more than one hundred people in the building and, after nine years in the field and working out of my home, this interaction challenged me to acquire new communication skills and techniques. My first job was to begin developing larger data processing accounts for banks, public utilities, hospitals and financial institutions.

Our first regional sales meeting was planned for August in San Jose, California. I called Dad with the news of my transfer and asked if he wanted a visitor for a few days. He was delighted. After the meetings ended, I caught a plane for Medford and was met by Dad and Vivian. I was a bit apprehensive because I was invited to stay with them and felt nervous about seeing his wife again. This time I was curious to compare his second choice with Mom and see how that marriage was working out for Dad.

They were excited about my visit and prepared a special roast beef dinner with champagne. We talked until midnight. I told them about the family and his grandchildren back home and how I had traveled alone to Oregon twelve years earlier, searching for him. I retraced my steps, telling about stopping at the Dexter Lake Club and asking the bartender if he knew Dad. Vivian's face lit up with surprise and she said, "I was there then! My sister and I ran the café and bar. If you had been there an hour earlier, we would have met and I could have told you about your Dad. He was working over on the coast and would come back on weekends." The effects of the wine helped me to tell her more about McCredie Springs, near Eugene, and how I found only a shell of a motel because of the fire. "Yes!" she said. "That happened just before we moved to Grants Pass. That place burned to the ground so we bought a motel here in town."

"Our home here was a rundown old farmhouse and your dad nearly rebuilt the whole place. After we moved in here, I told your dad if he wanted this marriage to last, he would have to find work closer to home." Dad just sat there listening and didn't say much.

Either the wine or the stress from the conversation was giving me a headache, so I closed the evening by telling them how happy I was to see them, said good night and went upstairs to bed. I felt like a kid again. "I'm in my dad's house! I can't believe this is happening. After 30 years, here we are, together again." I cried for a long time that night and welcomed the warm tears as they rolled down my cheeks. I thought, "Twelve years ago, I missed finding him by one hour. Surely God had other plans for me or He wouldn't have let that happen." I have a day and a half more with Dad. Will this be the time we talk, or will I wait for yet another time?"

The next morning we walked around the property and I listened to Dad talk about the mountains, the weather and more road-building stories. I was just fascinated by our being together and not yet enthusiastic about starting an intense conversation about our past family life. Timing is everything, and this still wasn't the time. After lunch, I listened to Vivian tell about growing up in the Mormon Church and about how strict her father was with the family.

"That was something we didn't have much of around our place," I thought.

She went on to show me some of her son's modeling pictures in *Playboy* magazine. She pulled out a year's worth of issues showing her son modeling Levi jeans. It made me remember when I was a kid selling magazines door to door in the spring before Dad moved west. I sold *Liberty, Saturday Evening Post,*

Colliers and *Life* magazines. One evening the man delivering them to me introduced *True* magazine for men. This was filled with adventure for men and bordered on the risqué. Dad didn't think I should be exposed to this information and told the delivery man to leave and take all his magazines with him. It seemed strange Dad didn't have anything to say then about Vivian's son! He just passed it off and giggled as Vivian turned the pages to find her son's pictures.

We ended the weekend on a pleasant note and I had to admit I really enjoyed our time together. We shared stories and had a lot of laughs. At times, I thought my need to get serious with Dad about our past might not be necessary. I couldn't spoil this weekend for either of us as this was the time to build our relationship. We were inseparable during the weekend. We climbed his mountain, fished in his pond, fed his chickens and cows and I got to drive the pickup to town. Sunday came much too soon and it was time to say goodbye. I promised them I'd be back again and boarded the plane.

The flight home was topped off by flying over two of my favorite places in the world, the mysterious and peaceful Crater Lake in Oregon and the majestic Mount Shasta in northern California. I remembered watching the mountain as we passed by it on the train after the divorce 20 years earlier. I was 19 then and thought my world had ended because I had no plans of ever seeing my dad again.

The Showdown

My next quarterly sales meeting ended after two days and I was tired. I had talked to our regional manager about marketing strategies, sales reports and operating budgets all day. I had a headache from too much wine during lunch and all I wanted to do was relax and wait for my plane back to Denver.

Being only 300 miles from Grants Pass, I battled with myself about whether or not to call Dad. "No, I'm too damned tired. I'm going home. Then again, he's nearly 73 and I'm about to hit the big 4-0. I haven't talked to him for several months and this would be a good time," I thought. "Why should I call him? He never calls me," I argued with myself. Then I whispered, "To hell with it, I've gotta call him!"

"Hi, Dad, how ya doing!," I said without waiting for an answer. "I've been down here in San Francisco for a sales meeting for a few days and am ready to head back to Denver. I'm at the airport. How's things in God's country?" I said, all in one breath. I was still feeling resentful about him always telling me Oregon was "God's country" because I thought "God's country" would be anywhere with a father who stayed home with his children. "The plane leaves in twenty minutes and I thought I'd give you a holler. How's Vivian?" I asked, stopping and taking a breath to give him a chance to answer all my questions. He hesitated long enough to alert me to listen to his answer.

"Ed, Vivian passed away after Christmas last year. It was her heart. We didn't know her heart was so weak until just before she died. It really happened fast. It's good to hear from you. When you're done with your meetings, is there any chance you could come up for a few days? It's easy to get cabin fever when I'm here alone. I'd sure like to see ya." "Sure, Dad, I'll be up! I'll check with the airlines to see when the next flight leaves San Francisco and call you right back. Dad, I'm really sorry to hear about Vivian."

I didn't know how to feel after hearing about Vivian. I had nothing against her and I even felt a little sorry for Dad. "This ought to be some weekend, just the two of us together with nothing to do but talk," I thought.

The next flight to Medford would leave in an hour. I changed my flight plans and called Pat. She too was shocked to hear about Vivian and encouraged me to go see Dad. "Everything's fine around here," she said. "Don't worry about us. Have a good time." Pat was always supportive of anything I did in regard to my reconciling with Dad. She had a great relationship with her father and wanted the same for me. I called Dad and told him about the flight and said I'd see him in two hours. Throughout the flight I wondered why Dad hadn't called to tell me his wife had died. I suspected he could still feel vulnerable to any criticism I might have of him if he tried to reach out to me. Dad asking me to come was the first time he ever needed anything from me.

It was dark when I pulled into his yard. The August night in Oregon was warm and the place was quiet. The cold beer and sandwich were little comfort for my headache. Our conversation went back to Vivian and her unexpected death. I recognized Dad's love for her and felt jealous he didn't have the same love for Mom.

The next morning I lay in bed listening to the wood snap and crack in the cookstove as I smelled the coffee and bacon. Dad's short-wave radio was blaring out the world news. I stayed in bed for a while, just drowning myself in good feelings about sleeping in my dad's house and delaying the urge to get up and start the day. "This is going to be my greatest day alone with

Dad so let's get it started," I said. With that, I jumped out of bed and was soon greeted with a hug and a cup of coffee.

After breakfast we went for a walk around the pond and up the mountain to check his fresh mountain water supply to make sure it was working.

As I looked out over the land, I realized neither my own imagination nor Hollywood's could arrange a more beautiful setting for a father-and-son walk. This experience was the fulfillment of my childhood dream. I remembered listening to Dad tell about the ranch we'd have someday in the mountains and how we would all be together and, here, part of that dream had come true.

I felt like a kid again and desired to run around the pond, lie down and roll around in the grass like a joyful child. I even thought about jumping into the pond. The child, the teenager and the adult inside were trying to get out to show my joy of being with my dad after so many lonely years apart.

We planned our day so we could visit Crater Lake National Park, a place I remembered from our trip to Oregon with Pat and the kids seven years earlier. Crater Lake is located in the crater of Mount Mazama, an inactive volcano in the Cascade Mountain Range. Geologists believe the lake was formed thousands of years ago when the top of Mount Mazama, then about 14,000 feet high, collapsed and was swallowed up inside the mountain. The collapse left a huge bowl which gradually filled with water. A small volcano called Wizard Island formed in the lake later when lava erupted from the interior of the mountain. The Klamath Indians believed the lake's waters had healing qualities and I wanted it to be true.

The lake is always still and seems eerie from the viewing stand, located a hundred feet above the lake shore. The wind may be raging in the forest above but down below, the lake remains undisturbed. The opposite was true with me. On the surface, I too presented a composed image to my father, but deep inside a storm was brewing.

We had lunch and then began the 60 mile drive back to Grants Pass. Dad fell asleep with his chin resting on his chest.

Again, I was feeling the excitement of seeing myself, driving along with Dad as though we had been doing this forever. I looked over at him and thought about all the years we had lost and the sharing of our lives we had missed along the way. I felt happy knowing we had lots of good times still ahead.

We stopped by to meet Judy, Vivian's sister, and invited her out to Dad's place for dinner. She appreciated the invitation and planned to see us at eight that evening. Dad and I shopped and prepared the grill for a big steak dinner, then waited for Judy. Judy wasn't as serious as Vivian and enjoyed my stories about my big family and all the craziness and fun Pat and I had raising a daughter and five sons. At that point I realized I didn't have to always be so intense and could enjoy some lighthearted talk.

Then Dad started talking, telling Judy about all our "dumb" relatives who stayed on their farms during the Depression and nearly starved to death. My anger began brewing from deep inside. He was talking about people I loved. I had spent my summers on their farms to fill in for the promise of a ranch Dad never provided. Judy, just listening, was probably bored. There was a lull in the conversation when Judy got up to pour some coffee, then she began asking about my mom.

She said, "Your mother must be a great lady to raise six children and have you all turn out so well." The feelings locked deep inside came to the surface. I could say, "Yeah, that's right," or I could share the truth. I hesitated to respond but knew I had to answer. I couldn't wait much longer or she would think I was rude and had ignored her question. "When is a good time to tell your dad what he did to you was wrong?" I thought. I could no longer stifle my anger. I could feel the adrenaline and could hardly breathe. I began to sweat. I told myself I had to be strong. Finally I made a choice. I couldn't let this opportunity pass.

"Yes, Judy, my mom is a great lady, and she did do a great job raising us six kids. She had to do it all alone because my dad ran out and left her alone and never came back!" By then I was burning up inside and Judy just sat there listening. I knew she was hearing things not heard before. She was only slightly aware of Dad's "other family" and I began to tell her the whole story. "Dad left home when I was nine. The night before he left home, he promised me he would come back for us and we would move to a ranch out west. Instead, he got lost somewhere between working and screwing around with other women. To make a long story short, my parents' whole goddamned relationship ended in divorce. My mother picked up the pieces, tried to keep some order in the family and helped us put our lives back together. Dad stopped supporting us and, for nine years, we didn't know if he was even alive."

I turned and faced Dad and asked, "Do you remember the time we spent together when I was five? Did you know how much I loved you? You were everything to me and the only person I felt close to then. I rode with you in the grader, we went swimming together and I was always around the shop. I didn't even know my brother and sisters and hardly remembered Mom because I was always with you. You were my whole life. I was always so lonesome for you and waited for you to come home. I could have done better in school and I wouldn't have been so resentful or into so much trouble. I would have tried more for you. I really missed you a lot, Dad. All my friends' dads were home with their kids and I told my friends about the great things you were doing out here. All the time I knew I was lying because, deep down, I knew you weren't coming back. You could have been there to help me decide what I wanted to do with my life. As it was, I had to make decisions and work out problems alone."

By then, I was sobbing in front of both of them but I needed to continue. I didn't care any longer about his feelings or what would happen to our relationship. I had to tell him everything. I was hurting so much. There was a knot in my stomach which had to be untied. I barely remember seeing Judy get up to go inside. I could see her through the window doing the dishes, and that's the last I remember of her. In the midst of my outburst she went home.

"Dad, I remember the remark you made to Mom at the divorce hearing about her refusing to move away from Omaha.

That hurt Mom a lot. I read every letter that came to the house and, never once, did you ask Mom to move or even mention any plans for us to move to Oregon. That was a goddamn lie. Mom had moved five times before you left home. Why wouldn't she move again? You didn't want us around and your behavior put us on welfare. I hated you for a long time after you left and, at times, I wanted to kill you for the pain you caused. She didn't deserve what you did to her. Judy was right. Mom is a great lady and, as close as I was to you and as much as I loved you, Mom is the one who deserves to be loved. She stayed home and fought it out through those tough years when we were all growing up. All my life has been spent wanting us to be together."

"Why didn't you come home, Dad?" I screamed.

I felt as if all my energy had been wrenched out of me. I kept on crying and believed I had made the wrong decision. I felt so alone and empty as I sat there looking across the valley with only a few farm lights twinkling. I guessed it was past midnight. I didn't have any more to say and just sat there sobbing.

I was sure this evening would be the last time I would see my dad and began to regret the remarks I had just made. He looked like a little boy who had just been punished. As tough as he was, I doubt if anyone ever confronted him about his behavior. I wondered why he didn't get up and take a swing at me or say something about a son who rips into his dad. Then I realized this encounter wasn't a little boy talking to his dad, but a confrontation between two grown men.

There was a long silence until one of us mumbled it was late and time for bed. As we walked to the door, I put my arm around his shoulder. Reaching the stairs we stopped, I turned to look at him, hugged him and said, "Good night, Dad!" He acknowledged my remark with an extra squeeze and smiled as I turned to go upstairs.

I awoke to the same radio station telling about world news and weather, only this time it wasn't so loud. The smell of coffee wasn't so strong and I could barely hear the wood snapping and cracking in the wood stove. I thought, "Oh God, everything was so great yesterday morning and everything is so bad this morning! I can't get up! I can't face Dad after last night. What am I going to say? I can't just pretend nothing happened last night."

"Lord," I prayed, "help me just to get through the kitchen door and the first two minutes with Dad and I'll give you my life forever!" I made a lot of extra noise getting dressed so he would at least know I was alive. I also let him think about what to say. "Mumbling seemed to work OK last night when we went to bed, so I'll just try it again," I thought.

"Good morning, Edward," he said first as I entered the kitchen.

"Wow!" I thought, "Things won't be so bad." I leaned over and gave him a hug and said, "Hey, good morning Dad!"

Our conversation was mixed. We talked about the Vietnam situation and politics. Nothing was said about the previous night and it was just as well. I was beginning to feel better and I didn't need to rehash anything with Dad about last night. I wanted to believe I had said everything I needed to. We enjoyed our ham and eggs breakfast and, over a third cup of coffee, I said, "Dad, tell me about my grandfather, your dad."

"Well, Ed, there isn't much to say. I didn't know him. I only remember walking along, holding his hand and wearing his ball cap. He left Omaha when I was five years old. He was a semi-pro baseball player for a team in St. Joseph, Missouri. He was gone a lot. He had red hair. His name was George Edward and he grew up in David City, Nebraska. He had lots of brothers and sisters and his father, Jacob Reinhardt, ran the general store. He moved to Denver and that's the last your Grandma and us kids ever heard of him. I was going through Denver one time before I met your mother and thought about looking him up, but I didn't. I suppose he's buried somewhere around Denver. That's about all I know."

I was shocked to learn his middle name. I always knew his first name was George, but didn't know his middle name was the same as mine—Edward. My anger left me that morning as I began to see how much we, as parents, influence the lives of our children. "Dad didn't have much to start out with," I thought.

"At least I had a good Christian mother who kept us together and really gave her life for us."

"Dad, would you come to Denver for a visit?" I asked. "I would really like for you to visit Pat and see the kids again."

"That would be great, Ed. I'd like to do that."

Dad's Homecoming

*T*he family was bubbling with excitement in preparation for Dad's visit to Denver a few months later. The novelty of having another grandpa and a character like Dad brightened their lives. Dad hadn't been around children much and some times his antics made me wonder who was the child and who was the adult. When he heard my kids crying about something, one of his favorite remarks was, "What ya laughin' about, Bub?" That question made them stop and realize they were not laughing. His offbeat remark sometimes stopped the crying—and sometimes made it worse.

Dad started calling me "gumshoe" after I told him I had located members of his father's "second" family in Denver just before his visit. He explained a "gumshoe" was an old slang word for a private detective or investigator. I wanted to tell him investigating and finding people was nothing new since I had spent so much of my life searching for him. I asked if he would like to meet his half-sister, Dorothy Wendelin, and her family. His other half-sister, Helen Boyd, lived in California and his half-brother, Patrick Thomas, had died several years before.

After some hesitation he agreed to meet Dorothy and we spent an afternoon with her. Dorothy had a box full of pictures of their father and told stories about his playing baseball and his work as a glazier for a glass company. It was interesting watching Dad listen to stories about his dad. He was unusually quiet and asked a few questions about his dad's being left-handed and having red hair. I felt a new closeness to both my grandfather and my father that afternoon. Being left-handed gave all three of us something in common. I felt sorry for my dad, listening only to stories about his dad and never having had the experience of knowing him. My love for Dad grew that afternoon and I quietly thanked God for the strength to find him and develop our relationship. We visited his father's grave in north Denver the following day and again I wondered what was going through his mind.

The bigger question I had on my mind all week was whether or not he wanted to drive to Omaha to visit the rest of the family. I told my siblings earlier he might agree to visit them if they all came home, but I wasn't sure. Two of them would make the trip from Chicago if he would agree.

Dad had not seen some of them in 30 years. When I asked, he agreed but was noncommittal about it. "Sure, if you want to," was his response. This indecisiveness about family matters sickened me. I took his response to mean he really didn't care. I buried my disgust and excused his behavior by thinking, "You can't give what you didn't receive."

Despite our growing relationship, I still experienced a lot of anxiety and fear about saying or doing something to upset him. It seemed like I was always trying to please him so he wouldn't get angry, especially at me.

My younger brother, Jim, had not seen Dad since the divorce, and the reunion party would be at Jim's house. Jim had never been afraid to express his opinion about anything and I was uncertain how he might react. I knew Dad was capable of saying something sarcastic while trying to be funny after having a drink or two. The sarcasm could start a fight.

Dad and I were within 50 miles of Omaha and I could feel the tension rise within me. With all the nerve I could muster, I decided to warn Dad of Jim's sensitivity about the past. "You and I have a good relationship, Dad. We can laugh and joke about most anything, but Jim has not been with you like I have. I would be a little careful when talking to him." Ten minutes after the introductions, they were walking around the house with Jim's arm over Dad's shoulder. The evening was a great success and I was proud of myself for making this reunion happen. "Why do I still worry so much?" I wondered.

My worrying wasn't over. Dad and I shared a room that night at my sister Bunny's place. While getting ready for bed, Dad stepped into the bathroom, leaving his suitcase opened on top of the bed. He had removed some clothing and I noticed two holstered pistols lying beside a shirt. "Thank God he didn't take them to the party," I thought. Nothing was ever said about the guns being a source of security for Dad, but the pistols were my clue of his fear and mistrust of other people, something I, too, struggled with all of my life.

During the years to follow, I continued my visits with Dad in Oregon, as did my siblings. On occasion, Mom would visit him with one of us. For most of my brothers and sisters, reconciliation between them and Dad had evolved from those visits. During one of them, Dad asked my sister Kitty and her two youngest children to come and live in Oregon with him. She had just ended her marriage of 25 years and needed time away from her home in Chicago. Kitty agreed and spent the next few years in Oregon where she completed her college education. While visiting Dad in 1982, I asked him if he would ever consider moving back home to Nebraska. I explained to him how Kitty was finishing college and, after five years in Oregon, was anxious to move closer to her other three children. Dad had just turned 80 and living alone without family support might be a problem. As the time drew nearer to Kitty's graduation, Dad decided to move back to Omaha. When I heard this, tears of joy began to well up inside me. My dream might finally be coming true. Dad was coming home!

In May of 1983, two of our sons, Tom, then 17, and Paul, 13, traveled with me to Oregon for the big migration back to Omaha. Others in the family volunteered to drive him home but I told them all, "No, this is my deal!" Tom would be the fourth driver and Paul was along to listen and challenge Dad on his biased and chauvinistic remarks about most anything including religion, politics, labor unions and Ford pickups. They would be a good match because Paul wouldn't let him speak in generalities. For example, Dad believed all ministers should have full-time jobs like everybody else and do their preaching on weekends or in their spare time.

Dad's Ford pickup and trailer had only canvas tops so he didn't think it would be safe to stop at night. His plan was to drive straight through to Omaha, a distance of nearly 2,000 miles. He figured I could drive at night and he would drive in the daytime. Just 30 minutes out of his town of Grants Pass, Oregon, I took over and realized I would be driving the rest of the way to Omaha. That is, except for the time when we were about 20 miles west of Laramie, Wyoming. Dad decided he wanted to drive on Interstate 80. The road was arrow straight with very little traffic and we could see for miles. I thought this was a safe place for him to drive so I encouraged him to take the wheel. Having only three hours of sleep out of the past 32, I closed my eyes.

A while later, I heard Dad say, "Ed, I can't see a damn thing!"

I jumped as I opened my eyes to see we had entered a tunnel about a quarter mile long. I said to him, "Steady Dad, you're doing fine!" I noticed we were still on the right side of the center line. "Just a little to the right, Dad, then hold it steady. You're doing OK! Now, back a little to the center. We're almost through."

"I'm sorry, Ed, I don't see too good in the dark," he confessed

I couldn't take the steering wheel from his hands because I wanted him to succeed in getting us out of the tunnel. It was the first time I saw him vulnerable and I felt so needed by him. He seemed so much like a child in this situation. After I calmed down, I suggested he take a break and, from then, I drove on into Omaha. After crossing the border into Nebraska, I counted another milestone in my struggle to find Dad and bring him home.

During the following year I made frequent visits to Omaha and spent lots of time with Mom and Dad. I enjoyed our dinners together and watched their interactions which gave me the feeling this arrangement was like old times. I wondered what they thought of me and my efforts to bring the family together. I cherished those visits, believing I had reached my goal and fulfilled my dreams of having the order I needed in my family, complete with a mom and a dad. Although Dad and Mom had a friendly relationship, they did not remarry nor live together. Dad continued living with my sister, Kitty, until his death in 1990 at the age of 89.

Going Through the Motions

𝕵n the summer of 1984, weeks before Eddie's accident and a year after Dad moved back to Omaha, I was nearing 51—the same age Dad was at the time of his divorce from Mom. I began thinking more about my own life and how much of my life had been consumed with my dream of bringing my parents back together. I began to realize how much I had been out of touch with reality during those years.

For years I had obsessed about my relationship with my father. My dream had been realized. I had a relationship with my father. He was back home and I could visit him any time I wanted. Shouldn't I be feeling freed since I'd accomplished my goal? I should, but I knew it was time to take stock of my relationship with my wife and children. For years I had gone through the motions of a proper life. I saw to it my kids were educated, I took them to church and supported all of their outside activities, but still had a void in my life.

"If there was ever a time to let go of him, isn't this the time? Isn't what I've done enough?," I thought. My behavior seemed like an addiction. At the time an addiction begins, the progress toward maturity is put on hold. When the addiction or obsession gets under control, or resolved, the person could find himself out of step and immature in his relationships. He discovers he has not grown emotionally while under the influence of the addiction. This is where I found myself. For example, I would say to Pat, "I don't feel like I'm 40, I feel like I'm 19." Interesting 19 was the age I was at the time of the divorce.

For years, when coming home from a social event, I would say to Pat, "There was no one at the party my age, or there was no one like me." Pat, irritated, would reply by reminding me of people who were our age and with similar circumstances to ours. Her rational response did nothing to ease the isolation and loneliness I felt.

I had been preoccupied for many years by a secret drama. Daydreaming played a big part in removing me from every day life. I loved movies and, before I was reconnected with my dad, Hollywood fueled my inner vision with pictures of horses, mountains, a ranch and Dad. Just the two of us.

After my reconciliation with him, my new desire was to bring Mom and Dad together. It didn't occur to me then I might be manipulating my parents to fulfill my needs for an idealized family structure. My relentless need was having order in my life. The fact I was still preoccupied with my birth family, after 20 years of marriage was significant. All along, I thought I was doing what was best for everyone, even helping God answer my prayers.

Keeping secrets was another way my family coped with the difficulties of life. It seems, by keeping secrets, we're able to preserve our images before others. Within a year after my parents' divorce, I was visiting my aunt in O'Neill and she asked, "Did your folks get divorced when you were in Oregon?" I felt comfortable answering "Yes." Later my mother expressed her disappointment in me. "I wish you hadn't told them about the divorce. They don't need to know that." Did she think they would never find out?

Then I would turn around and use the same secret approach when I lied on job applications. For years I listed my father as deceased. Surely an employer would think better of me if my father died than if he abandoned me. Even after I got the letter from the license bureau in Oregon, listing Dad's address, I kept that secret too. I couldn't bear to tell Mom I had discovered he was married, even though we always assumed he was.

For some reason after I was married, I found it necessary to keep secrets from my wife. She would ask to see my paycheck and I would only show her the largest of my commission checks. For a long time I was ashamed of my salary. I was unable to accept that reality. My wife would ask, "How much is enough money for you?" For me, money was a substitute for self-esteem.

My wife would learn about other secrets, too. One day while I was out of town, a policeman came to the door with a summons for my 34 unpaid parking tickets. Other surprises came in the form of over-drafts from the bank and disconnected utilities. One of the biggies was accepting a transfer to another state without consulting my wife.

Having reached my only goal, I was now faced with the question of what to do with the rest of my life. It seemed like the situation in which I grew up prevented me from ever choosing a career. Survival was my sole motivation for making decisions about my work life. I resented the fact I had always struggled to make money but had never made a career choice.

Nothing seemed the same anymore. Nothing seemed to mean anything. I questioned my own worth and wondered what value I was to the family. I didn't seem to have a purpose in life. I felt irritated and depressed about the direction my life was taking. I felt I could no longer work just for the sake of earning an income. I was finding less and less strength to fight off those thoughts. I believed I would yield to them, let them take over and follow in Dad's footsteps, the same way he followed in those of his father. I kept telling myself I was just like both of them and neither counseling nor any other kind of help would change the direction of my life.

One day I was shocked when I realized my actions were reminding me of Dad before he left home. I remembered how he took me to the Sears store one Saturday morning for tennis shoes. Buying the shoes caused Dad to be irritated and upset.

He didn't talk to me all the way home. I thought it was my fault he was angry at me.

I began to question my relationship with my wife and thought she was the cause of my unrest. We had been seeing marriage counselors off and on for the past five years and nothing ever got solved. I had no idea what Pat wanted from me and I was convinced I was a good husband and father. Wasn't I doing everything a husband and father should do to support his family and protect his children? Finally, we began seeing two counselors at once, a man and a woman. They agreed with Pat that I hadn't made an emotional commitment to the family, insisting I was still holding back from being a real part of the family. I didn't know what the hell they were talking about.

I told Pat it seemed as if I was standing in a river and the water was rising. I felt it would soon sweep me off my feet and I would be carried away. I told her I believed the history of divorce in my family was pulling me away from the marriage.

My thoughts about leaving the family continued into the summer. Then, just days before Eddie's accident, I began making plans to leave. "Well," I thought, "with five sons playing football and twenty-five games to attend, this would be a poor time to leave."

I had planned over a year for the "Reinhardt family big game," the Colorado-Nebraska game to be played in Colorado. I had forty-two tickets for our relatives and friends. We would have John on the Nebraska side of the field and Eddie playing for Colorado. "No father would miss an opportunity to watch two of his sons play in the biggest game of the family's football career. I can't leave now," I concluded.

The irony that caused me much distress was the fact that my dad was 51 and I was 19 at the time of the divorce, and I was 51 and Eddie was 19 when he was injured in the very same town.

Reaching Out to Touch Eddie

I felt the plane touch down in Portland. For an instant I felt confused about where I was and why I was on this plane. Immediately, the thought of Eddie grabbed my stomach so tightly, I could barely breathe. For many months afterward I would live with this feeling of panic each morning upon awakening. It would become my daily reminder nothing would ever be the same, a reminder each day would bring new and more critical problems to solve. It would remind me of what is important and what is incidental in life.

"Are you Mr. Reinhardt?"

I opened my eyes and saw a tall man in uniform leaning directly over my head. It was one of the pilots. He located my seat right after we stopped at the gate to tell me some news. I was startled and nearly jumped out of my seat.

"Yes, I'm Ed Reinhardt."

"I understand you're on your way to Eugene, Oregon, to be with your son who was injured during a football game this afternoon," he said quietly.

"Have you heard something about my son?" I asked.

"No, I don't have any news about him, but we did receive a message for you from our office in Portland. Word from the University of Oregon athletic department was passed on to us that your wife and two children are on their way from Lincoln, Nebraska, and will be in Eugene in a few hours. That's all I know."

I thanked him for the news about Pat and the kids and told him what a relief it was to know we would soon be together.

"Another thing," he said, "an Oregon alum, a Mr. George Lamont, will be waiting for you at the gate in Portland. He will fly you to Eugene in his private plane, so look for a man in a green jacket wearing an Oregon Ducks ball cap." As he turned to leave, he added, "I hope your son will be all right."

A man wearing the described attire was standing at the gate as Nelse and I filed into the waiting area. As I looked at him, I felt frightened of what I would soon hear about Eddie. This man's expression told me he was part of the tragedy and, as our eyes met, we each knew we had found the right person. We stepped toward each other with outstretched hands.

"Yes, I'm Ed Reinhardt and this is my friend, Nelse Hendricks. You're George Lamont. We were just told by the pilot to meet you here at the gate." Before we moved, I asked him, "Do you have any news about my son, Eddie."

He said, "Eddie was just leaving surgery as I was leaving the hospital to pick you up. The last I heard was he was moved into the recovery room."

Nothing more was said. He explained where his plane was located and asked us to follow him.

I remember only hallways and stairs and stepping through several doors until we were walking outside to the plane. I tried to stifle my feeling of terror by holding on to every word he said about the takeoff and by listening to him as he talked to the air traffic controller.

George made a special effort to keep my mind busy by explaining all pre-flight activities. It was after ten at night and the sky was clear over Portland. Once we were airborne, George picked out several landmarks and was enthused to point out the city lights and the outline of the beautiful Columbia River. He talked about the origin of its name, its length and its usefulness to the city and to the state of Oregon. We were less than a mile high and were looking at one of the most brilliant starry skies I could remember.

"What kind of work do you do, George?" I asked, hoping to get my mind on something else. "I raise chickens," George replied. "I own the Lamont Featherland Farms in Colburg, Oregon. We raise about 11 million chickens a year. At a certain age the chickens are shipped down to California to egg-laying stations and the eggs are then distributed to the public through grocery stores."

"Wow!" I thought, trying desperately to think of something to say back. "My grandmother raised chickens too, but she didn't fly around in an airplane. Gram raised less than 500 chickens per year." I couldn't muster up anything more clever to say so I let him continue his discourse about his work and his airplane and his association with the University of Oregon. He had graduated from Oregon and then became a fighter pilot during the Korean conflict. I realized later he would have been a student at the university at the time of my parents' divorce.

Earlier that afternoon, George met with the coaching staff to plan how to bring me to Eddie. George had volunteered to pick us up in Portland and to fly us to Eugene. "Have you ever been to Oregon, Ed?" George asked.

"Yes," I answered sadly, "I was in Eugene a long time ago." George didn't pursue my response and I didn't say more.

George pointed out the landing lights off in the distance. At the far end of the runway, lights formed what appeared to be a cross.

I thought, "How far away the Lord seems to be on this night." I wondered if the cross was meant to be a reminder to me of His presence in my life and pondered if all I had to do was ask Him to lift my burden of fear and anxiety from what I was about to face.

After landing, George taxied the plane down an alleyway to his parking garage and shut off the engine.

"Will you guys help me push the plane into the garage? One can get behind the tail and Ed, you push the other wing." I was surprised how easily it moved. George locked the door and we walked a block and a half to the terminal parking area. While walking to the car, I thought back to the start of this day, never dreaming I'd be pushing an airplane at midnight.

The ten mile drive to the hospital was the last part of this journey and it seemed to be taking forever. We had moved so close but now I could barely face it.

To help break the tension, I said, "George, would you mind staying on Interstate 5 and driving into California for a while? I'm not ready to go into the hospital yet." George ignored my meager attempt at humor and drove quietly on. As we entered the city, we passed by the old neon sign I remembered from long ago, lighting the night skies with the words "EUGENE HOTEL."

Finally, we made our way through the hospital lobby to the elevator which would take us to the intensive care unit on the fifth floor. The three of us were silent as the elevator, click by click, moved upward. I struggled with the fear of hearing the doctor say Eddie was gone. Having that door open would be the most frightening moment of my life. Panic was causing my heart to beat faster and the lump in my throat made me gasp for breath. The door opened and the first person I recognized was Eddie's coach, Bill McCartney. Coach Mac was talking to three other men directly in front of the elevator. Instantly, I searched their eyes for the words I dreaded to hear. Before stepping off the elevator, I looked out to Coach Mac for some sign about Eddie. "He's still alive," were the words I heard as I reached out to shake his hand. "Eddie is still alive and has been stable since the operation," repeated Coach McCartney.

He introduced me to two of the other men and, while I tried to be polite, all I wanted to do was go to Eddie. I shook hands with them. Before meeting the last gentleman, I cried out, "Where is my son? I need to see my son!" Little more was said as they led us through the large double doors into intensive care. I could barely keep from screaming out his name. Finally, we reached his dimly lit room. After being with him a few minutes, my fears began to wane. "I am here with you, Eddie, and I'll do everything I can to help keep you alive." I felt like I had some control of my fear that Eddie was going to die.

Looking over his large, long body, bare from the waist up, a peacefulness come over me. All I wanted was to touch him and to tell him I was with him. As I slowly moved toward his bed, I could feel my stomach twist with fear. Because of the maze of wires covering his body, there was no place to touch him except high on his shoulders and on his cheeks. His head was completely bandaged except for his face. An oxygen tube was in his nose and ran down along his cheek. Monitors covered his body, leading up to screens above his head where continuous beeps reported some bodily function; others reported his condition by flashing white lines across a screen which abruptly ended with a loud beep. The wires were scrambled over his massive chest, keeping me from leaning over to hold him. Coach Mac was standing by my side and touched me on the shoulder.

Eddie's whole body would tighten every minute or so and his hands would grip so tightly the nurse had placed rolls of cloth in his hands so he wouldn't cut the palms of his hands with his fingernails. This wrenching and twisting, similar to a seizure, would continue for the next few days. "My God," I thought, "what is happening to Eddie?"

We stood there quietly for nearly ten minutes before Coach Mac said anything. Finally, he began discussing the results of the surgery as reported to him by the doctor earlier. "A blood vessel on the left front side of his brain burst as a consequence of a tackle. They had to remove the blood clot and stop the bleeding. They believe the operation was successful. The doctors think Eddie has a good chance to live." The coach continued in a calm, caring voice, "The doctors said the continual stiffening of his body is not unusual after brain surgery. It's the body's reaction to this kind of abuse to the brain. The doctors predict the next 24 hours will be the most critical. If he makes it through this, his chances of making it will get better. All we can do is pray and wait."

"I know how to wait," I thought.

Before leaving Eddie's room, Coach McCartney prayed for my son's survival this night and for recovery from such a serious injury. I could feel the spiritual energy fill my body as we stood side by side. After praying together, we stepped out of the room and talked again to the other three men I had seen at the elevator. Later that night, as my family collected at Sacred Heart Hospital, Coach Mac would take each of us into Eddie's room. He prayed Eddie would survive and we would have the strength to endure what was ahead for all of us.

Dr. Bill Lawton, the team doctor for the University of Oregon and one of the three men standing by the elevator when I arrived, had been at the hospital with Eddie since late afternoon. His confidence and gentle spirit reassured me every possible step had been taken to save Eddie's life. He too, reminded me of how critical the first 24 hours were and how Eddie's chances could improve after that time. Herb Yamanaka, the second man, expressed with great tenderness how sad he felt about the accident. He was an assistant athletic director at the university and was assigned to be available to us for whatever we needed. Later that evening, Herb assured me Eddie was in the arms of Jesus. He was the first person to tell me Eddie would not die.

Finally, the third person (the man I didn't wait to meet earlier) was standing there with his arms open, waiting to hold me so I could let go of everything I'd been holding back through this long day. What seemed like a long time in the arms of Reverend John Rohrbaugh was enough to regain some of my strength and to be assured God was caring for Eddie. I felt better meeting them, all so concerned about Eddie. As always, my friend Nelse stood by my side, strong and silent.

An Oregon Family Reunion

My first visits with Eddie were limited to 15 minutes, twice an hour. The remaining time was spent in the waiting room down the hall. I began to hear more of the details about the accident from Coach McCartney, Herb Yamanaka and Dr. Lawton. Coach Mac explained how several members of the coaching and medical staff had reviewed the game film. He assured me there was no illegal tackle and the injury was an accident. Dr. Lawton told me a drug called Mannitol was administered immediately after Eddie collapsed. This drug shrinks the brain until the blood clot can be removed. Without Mannitol, pressure on the brain stem might stop his vital functions. Dr. Lawton said, "At no time did Eddie ever stop breathing."

It began to dawn on me two Oregon players were involved in the tackle in which Eddie was injured. I tried to imagine how they must feel. Herb told me about those two young men and their outstanding athletic and academic careers at the university. They had visited with Herb at the hospital shortly before I arrived and he told them Eddie had made it through the operation. They asked Herb to pass along their sympathy to Eddie's family.

I was alone with Eddie during my second visit. I had never been in an intensive care unit in my life. The monitors were keeping vigil as they continually reported his vital statistics were staying within normal ranges. The noisy respirator pumped air into Eddie's lungs until I thought they would burst then, with a pop, released for a moment and started over. "Why a respirator?" I wondered. "Isn't he able to breathe on his own? Is this a pre-caution or if they remove it will he stop breathing? Would he die? Is his only salvation from dying this machine? Would he ever breathe on his own again?"

"How long will we wait before we know anything about any disabilities he might suffer? Is he just still asleep from surgery, or is this what they call a coma?" Brain injury was a foreign concept to me. What does it mean? What's *injured*? Orthopedic injuries were common in the family—broken collar bones, a bro-ken jaw, sprained ankles and wrists, but this was entirely different! What does *injured really* mean? What will the next couple of days be like? Damn the watching and waiting and talking to all of those people! I took a deep breath and stood there looking at him with his eyes closed. I was waiting for the next tightening and shuddering of his body, which the nurse called posturing. I prayed the spasms would end.

My time with Eddie was up again. As I entered the waiting room, Nelse told me Pat, John and Rosemarie had landed in Eugene and would arrive at the hospital in a short while. Nelse remained with me and was the only person who really knew and understood my history. He had heard the story about my dad many times when we talked about our fathers over a beer after work.

During my next visit a nurse stepped in and told me my family had arrived. I let go of Eddie's shoulder and hurried to the waiting room to find Pat and the kids talking to Coach McCartney. We held each other for a long time then drew John and Rosemarie nearer to us and cried. Slowly, we began to talk about Eddie and to listen to Coach McCartney explain more of the details of the accident and what went on here at the hospi-tal. I introduced the family to Dr. Lawton and Herb Yamanaka. Soon we were all talking, sharing how we heard about the acci-dent and our flights to Eugene. Dr. Lawton briefed us about details of the operation and then shared the story of the neuro-surgeon, Dr. Arthur Hockey.

"Dr. Hockey is a big Oregon fan and was at the game. He sat behind and up from the Colorado bench. He noticed, when Eddie got up after being tackled in his last play, he seemed to be wobbling as he ran off the field. He watched Eddie collapse at the bench right in front of him. He got up and ran down to the field, introducing himself to the medical team who had gathered around Eddie. He contacted the hospital from the ambulance, directing them to prepare for emergency tests and possible surgery. When the ambulance arrived the x-ray staff and the surgical team were ready. Eddie was lucky," he said.

Herb started telling about the last few minutes of the game and the ride to the hospital in the ambulance. "There were only a few points difference in the score, so everybody stayed until the end. Hardly anyone left the stadium, which kept the bridge over the Willamette River clear of fans. This bridge is the only way back to the city and ordinarily it would have been filled with people. We were only minutes away from the hospital," Herb said.

Gaining information and being with my family eased my anxiety.

During the next visit to see Eddie, Pat and I stood together. We said nothing for a long time and finally Pat said, "Let's pray for Eddie." While raising our six children, prayer always helped bring us together to accept whatever problem we faced. Pat didn't hesitate to reach out to God to save Eddie's life. Her faith never wavered. I felt a closeness to Pat as I realized this wasn't just my child who was so close to death, but hers too.

Pat and I first took John and Rosemarie in to see their brother and explained the posturing movements. Pat explained this condition was not unusual after brain injury. I said a prayer, thanking God for her nursing background and her familiarity with this environment. We stood there trying to hold on to any part of his body which was free of wires and monitors until we were told our visit was over.

Some of those in the waiting room were beginning to doze off while others were quietly visiting. Pat and I decided one of us would be with Eddie at all times and developed a routine which would go on for several days. Only for unavoidable circumstances would both of us leave him unattended. Days and weeks went by at Sacred Heart Hospital in Eugene with one of us always by his side. Medical personnel were curious and amazed at our strength and dedication toward the care of our son.

Morning brought a safe feeling to me when I awakened to find nearly every sofa and chair filled with people sleeping and John and Nelse stretched out on the floor. I was told Coach McCartney had left the hospital to go for a walk. I was later told Coach Mac was seriously troubled by Eddie's accident. He questioned himself about whether any good comes from playing such a violent sport. He told a reporter he needed to re-establish his purpose for coaching. He felt like he might make changes in his life because of the part injuries play in this game, especially since something so tragic had happened to one of his players.

The doctors started making their rounds early in the morning and we were soon introduced to Dr. Arthur Hockey, the neurosurgeon who had operated on Eddie the night before and was in charge of his care. I was grateful for his kindness to Eddie. Dr. Hockey began by reviewing the operation with us in detail, explaining what he believed caused the injury. He had also reviewed the game film, running it slowly back and forth and agreed with the coaches that Eddie's head hit the tackler's thigh pad as his body was falling, just as the Oregon player's leg was coming up. His head then hit the ground very hard. "It was the acceleration-deceleration, or the sudden stopping of his head which caused the blood vessel to burst," he said. "The impact caused Eddie's brain to rush forward against the wall of the skull and then bounce back to the rear of the skull, causing damage to the brain. The extent of damage to the brain is unknown. Only after his awakening from the coma will we discover the extent of the injury." He explained how the flow of blood from the vessel was stopped and all blood was removed from the damaged area.

He emphasized he did not see anything to indicate a previous injury had caused the problem. There had been a question about a possible previous injury because Eddie had complained of headaches to a teammate during the game.

Dr. Hockey explained the uncertainty of how long the coma would last. "Of course, the longer his coma, the less likely he will have a full recovery."

"Now begins the greatest lesson in patience, trust and hope I will ever experience, in a city where I learned many other life lessons a long time ago, the least of which was trust," I thought.

On the morning following the injury, Mass in the hospital chapel was scheduled for ten o'clock and, as best we could, we prepared to go without a change of clothes or even a razor. Coach McCartney stayed with us throughout the day and provided the support we needed. He was the source of strength for all of us that day, always available for comfort or just to talk. Frequently he spent time with Eddie, praying for him and telling him over and over to keep fighting to live and not to give up, that Jesus was by his side, caring for him and loving him. If Eddie could hear our voices, no other person, not even I, his own father, could inspire and encourage him to hold on to life and keep fighting to stay alive as Coach McCartney could.

After Mass, Pat and I started taking turns phoning our relatives and answering incoming calls. I started by calling my brothers and sisters to give them more information about Eddie's condition. My sister Bunny and my brother Jim said they would relay the news to Dad about the injury. I could easily talk to Mom about Eddie because we had a close relationship, strengthened by working through our shared problems in the past.

Dad was a different story. Since our reconciliation, I had never gone to him with a problem. Now I needed him to help me through the worst tragedy of my life. I was feeling anxious about what I would say to him. "Should I just tell him what happened to Eddie and then just listen for some consolation or advice?" I wondered.

Bunny had talked to Dad and told him Eddie was hurt. When I called, our conversation started out on a serious tone. We normally began our phone calls with a couple of jokes about politics or something going on in the news. This time, he was soon swearing about the game of football and telling me how unfair life can be to nice guys like Eddie. I felt sorry for both of us when he said he wanted to be here in Eugene with us. I told him I wished he were here, too. Our talk ended when he told me to stay with Eddie, exclaiming, "Hang in there, Ed!" I was encouraged by this and went back to tell the kids about our conversation. I felt good after talking to Dad, just realizing I could go to him anytime for help. I wanted to believe, no matter how old I was, he would always be my father. I found comfort in that.

It's Easier to Give Than to Receive

Sunday after lunch, Herb Yamanaka and a friend came to visit. Herb asked me if we could talk for a moment. He introduced his friend as a sales manager from Dunham Oldsmobile in Eugene. The man expressed his sympathy about Eddie and wished him a quick recovery. I welcomed his kind words, curious about the reason for his visit. Herb suggested we talk away from the ICU waiting room, so the three of us moved down the hall. He said, "Mr. Reinhardt, I would like to help you and your family. I know you have several children and you will need transportation to get them around the city. You could be here for a while. I have two cars down in the parking lot for you to use for however long you're in town."

I was embarrassed someone outside the family would have to offer us a solution for our transportation needs. I began to sweat. I was too proud to ever ask for help, so this generous offer which might have pleased another person, seemed like a hand-out to me.

The man was waiting for my response and I just stood there, trying to figure out how I could decline his offer without hurting his feelings. I told him I could rent or lease the cars but I couldn't just use them. His offer made me feel inadequate about taking care of my family. I also felt resentful about appearing needy. Somehow, common courtesy won out over my stubbornness and I responded graciously. "Thank you. I really appreciate your kindness," I mumbled.

Coach McCartney kept in touch with his coaching staff and they reported the flight back to Colorado was extremely quiet. The players were hurting for their teammate. Some could barely talk as they expressed their feelings privately to their position coaches about their friend, Eddie.

By Sunday afternoon, our son Tom, arrived with his high school football coach, Bernie McCall. Coach McCall had been at Heritage High School for several years and had coached some of our older kids. He was a former football standout at the University of Colorado and knew all about our family. It was good to see Tom and his presence helped further strengthen us.

The Sunday evening report from Dr. Hockey changed little from his remarks at noon. He thought the tightening of Eddie's body was becoming less frequent, which was a good sign.

Coach McCartney decided he would leave Eugene early Monday morning. Before leaving the hospital he prayed for Eddie and encouraged us to remain strong. We thanked him for staying over and told him how much his encouragement meant to us. I tried to say something to support him for the week ahead as he would go home to prepare his team to meet the incomparable personification of college football, Notre Dame University in South Bend, Indiana. I told him I couldn't imagine what it would be like to face a team like Notre Dame after the weekend he had been through.

On Monday evening Paul and Matt came out with Bob Neilsen, another Heritage coach. Finally, we were all together.

Pat and I continued our vigil with Eddie while John and Rosemarie monitored the telephone calls and visitors. Flowers and fruit baskets were arriving hourly, filling the waiting room. Flowers were not allowed in intensive care so volunteers delivered them to other patients. The people in Eugene continued their generous hospitality, offering anything we might need. Eventually, the kindest thing they could do was to tell us they believed Eddie would survive. I desperately wanted to believe.

The president of the University of Colorado, Arnold Weber, arranged for Dr. Glenn Kindt, director of neurosurgery for the University of Colorado Health Sciences Center, to come to Eugene. Dr. Kindt arrived Monday evening. His consultation with Dr. Hockey lasted several hours. Near midnight they decided to place a brain pressure monitor inside Eddie's head. They believed it should not wait until morning. This surgery continued a long succession of operations for our son.

Following the early morning surgery, Eddie was back in his room by 2:30 A.M. with yet another monitor for us to watch. The nurse explained the safety zones and what normal brain pressure was, so I held my breath and prayed each time it went above normal. "Go down, go down, go down!" I repeated as the beeper sounded and the white line raced across the screen.

At some point we began to assume he could hear us, so all conversations were directed to him in a positive tone. From then on we discouraged anyone from discussing his prognosis in his presence. Some were surprised by our assertiveness but followed our wishes.

We had arranged to call Coach McCartney each morning to give him a progress report. That way he would have the latest information from us for his athletic staff and for the media. During our first telephone conversation he told me what an impact Eddie's accident and his condition were having on the students and the people of Boulder and Denver. "You can't imagine all the calls I get from the community and from across the nation asking about him and his family. People are eager to help and have been asking if they can send money for expenses. Many letters have arrived with donations enclosed. My staff and the office of student affairs along with the Buff Club and alumni people want me to ask you if they can start an emergency fund for Eddie."

I was stunned by his request and hesitated to answer him right away. Again, I experienced a feeling of helplessness about meeting my family's needs. This attacked the very core of my worth to my family. I had decided I would never need or accept help from anyone. Now I could see my decisions being threatened through a situation I couldn't control.

I told him I wasn't sure but I would talk it over with Pat. He said to think it over and we could talk about it on Saturday. He said he and his wife, Lyndi, were coming to Eugene to see Eddie after the football game at Notre Dame. By the time I hung up the receiver, I had already decided I didn't need to talk to anybody about an emergency fund because I had just made my decision. We didn't need anybody's money. Eddie was covered by two accident insurance policies and I remembered Coach McCartney, the night he recruited Eddie, clearly telling us Eddie would also be insured by the University of Colorado. Other coaches recruiting him told us the same story. "What else would we need money for?" I thought. "Travel expenses for our trips to Oregon, some big phone bills, motel costs and a few business trips back to my office in Littleton. That's all! I don't need their charity!" How wrong I was.

Soon after I had talked by telephone with Coach McCartney, and before I was able to discuss the matter with Pat, I was called out of Eddie's room by Tom Lawry, the director of media relations for the hospital. Tom advised us about working with the media and prepared us for our first national press conference.

His approach was similar to Coach McCartney's just a few minutes earlier and his question was nearly the same. "Mr. Reinhardt, many people in the community, and at the University, are concerned about your financial needs during your time in Oregon. They want to start a fundraiser for the Reinhardt family." He said I didn't have to answer now, suggesting I talk it over with Pat and get back to him after the weekend.

I stopped in the cafeteria for a cup of coffee and to think. I was feeling terrible and just wished they would stop asking me questions. I was beginning to see the walls I had built up in this very city were crumbling and I could no longer keep people away from helping my family, the very thing I swore I would never let happen. I believed if I let my guard down and let people help me, then what I feared most, my inability to support my family, would make me a failure.

I decided my conversation with Pat about this matter would be short. I had plenty of reasons for saying *no* to any fund raising. Pat listened to me ramble on about all the reasons we didn't need their money. I was surprised at her calmness. Finally, when I had tired enough for her to say something, she quietly remarked, "You know, Ed, this money won't be for you, it will be for Eddie. He may need it someday to take care of himself. You do what you think best. . . you decide."

Late Saturday evening, Pat and I picked up Coach and Lyndi McCartney, and as we drove back to the hospital, Coach said to keep our eyes on Jesus and He would see all of us through the hard times.

I was silent as I drove, needing to listen to this man talk with strength and love from the Lord. I could feel my spiritual well, nearly emptied by the stress of the past week, begin to fill as we talked about the love Jesus had for Eddie and how He cared for Pat and me. He told us of the reports he had received about how strong we had been the preceding week, how special we were to be Eddie's parents and how fortunate Eddie was to have us. He didn't say much about his 55 to 10 defeat at Notre Dame. Maybe his faith and trust in Jesus were enough to carry him through the dark days as a coach at Colorado. Maybe he could visualize the great victories he would have in the future, like Colorado beating Nebraska, four years later, after 27 years of losses. I was beginning to feel the strain from the week and let go of my feelings as the tears fell on my jacket. All I could do was squeeze Pat's hand and listen.

We entered Eddie's room after midnight to hear his condition had not changed. On and on the monitors clicked and buzzed, telling us Eddie was fighting for his life and there was no sign of waking from the coma. The doctors told us pneumonia could become a greater threat to his life than his brain injury.

Then Coach McCartney spoke to Eddie with authority telling him he must keep fighting for his life and must never give up. He told Eddie about his teammates and the people back in Colorado, all praying for him. He said, "Over 150 million Americans know about you and your battle to recover. Don't give up!"

Mrs. McCartney stood by his side as he spoke while Pat and I were at the head of the bed, touching Eddie's face. Coach's encouragement reached me and I believe the message from this godly man reached Eddie, too.

After Coach McCartney's last visit with Eddie on Sunday morning, we had a chance to talk about the efforts made to start an emergency fund back in Colorado. By now, I had spent a few days reinforcing my beliefs of being able to pay our own expenses, having plenty of insurance and not needing their money.

I stepped out in the hallway and started looking out the window.

Suddenly, it was 1955 again, three years after my parent's divorce. I could hear my mother making a request. "Ed, would you drive me to the county court house?" "Sure Mom, what's going on?" I answered. "I have decided to apply for a government program for Jim. It's called Aid for Dependent Children."

A few weeks later, I sat next to my petite mom in the welfare office. She looked out of place in a hat, dress and high heels, nervously answering questions. "How long since the boy's father sent you any money? When was the divorce? Why isn't he sending you money now? Do you work?"

Embarrassed and humiliated to be asking for help from the county, I could feel my anger toward my father rising. "Money!" Money was always the god-damned problem, or so it seemed to me. The two things I vowed I would do when I had a family was to protect them from getting hurt and always provide what they needed.

Back at the hospital, it was becoming clear my vows were no longer appropriate after I started listening to Coach McCartney.

In a quiet voice, he talked about his coaching experience at Michigan and the number of injuries he remembered and how some injuries prevented players from ever playing football again. "What's ahead for Eddie at this time is unknown to anyone. The doctors don't have the least idea about the outcome of his injury and it could take months or years of rehabilitation. As a rule, most injuries are overcome in a short time, but God only knows how long this recovery may be. In fact, Eddie may never fully recover and may need financial support for the rest of his life. Your immediate expenses of five or six thousand dollars may be within your ability to pay, but if this recuperation goes on for long, it could be ten or twenty or a hundred times that amount. Eddie will need that kind of help, and he deserves it."

"Another purpose for the fund is to let the people of Boulder and Denver and the people in Colorado become part of his recovery. You know, they were just becoming acquainted with your son and finding him to be a good kid and a good football player. He got a lot of attention last week setting a new record for catching passes and, now, his being struck down has saddened a lot of people. They need to feel part of this battle. They can't stand over Eddie's bed like you and Pat, and they're hurting too. They want to help."

It became obvious to me, listening to him, just how selfish I had been about the whole matter. I recognized the pattern of my responses to people's kindness this past week—and for most of my life, for that matter—had been wrong. "This has nothing to do with me." I discovered. "They just want to help Eddie."

Quietly, I turned from the window, looked back at Coach and said, "I believe you're right, Coach. It's OK to go ahead with the emergency fund for Eddie. I'm sorry I couldn't tell you sooner; I had to work through some things myself. It would be an honor for us to have them help our son. I would really appreciate their help."

Early Monday morning I stopped in to see Tom Lawry with an answer to his question about the fundraiser for Eddie in Eugene. "Tom," I said, "financially, we're going to be OK. We have plenty of family insurance for medical expenses, along with the athletic department's insurance. Coach McCartney just told me they were raising money for Eddie back home and I have the money for our expenses here in Oregon. Many people from Eugene have been coming to the hospital to talk to us and to pray for Eddie. Tom, that's plenty for us. We don't need any more than that."

Tom accepted my decision and then added. "The Holiday Inn wants you to move to their motel. They have two rooms reserved for you and your family and you may stay as long as necessary. Would you be open to moving to the Holiday Inn?"

"Yes, Tom," I replied, "we'd really appreciate that. Are you sure they want us to stay until Eddie goes home? That could be several weeks."

"That's not a problem," he said.

I left Tom's office feeling much closer to the people of Eugene. More and more I found myself agreeing with Dad when he called Oregon "God's country."

Death's Door

*T*hree days had passed since Eddie's accident and the news reports in Denver continued to list him in critical condition with no change. They reported the insertion of the brain monitor as a minor setback. No one in the hospital would budge on giving a prognosis. The only hope and encouragement came from those faithful people around the country who showed great courage by telling us they believed Eddie would survive this tragedy. My faith wasn't strong enough to take the risk of believing. It was easier to live in fear of uncertainty and constant anxiety than to risk reaching out for this peacefulness they had by trusting the Lord. I had a lot to learn about trusting in the love of Jesus.

By Wednesday afternoon, John, Rosemarie and Tom were making plans to go back to their schools and we decided Paul and Matt would stay with us until the weekend. Since we were all going off in different directions with an assortment of emotions, Pat and I decided we should all meet with the hospital chaplain to express our feelings. We were not sure how to begin and we didn't know what to expect. Father Berg prayed with us and talked about the pain and suffering we had experienced as a result of the upheaval in our family. I could barely say a word without crying. Each mentioned something they missed about Eddie and spoke about a recent experience they had with him.

One of our favorite stories occurred when Eddie worked construction one summer. Early one morning family members saw him lining up slices of bread across the table. He topped each with a slice of meat and cheese. As he placed the top slices of bread on the dozen plus sandwiches, his brother asked about his large lunch. He replied shyly, "John, some guys I work with don't have enough money to buy lunch after Wednesday and pay day is Friday. Do you mind if I help them out?"

Eddie had touched people we didn't yet know about. Several months after we returned from Oregon with Eddie, I was removing his belongings from his college dorm room in Boulder. I had made several trips from his room to the pickup and had passed a janitor in the hallway several times, occasionally greeting him or making a comment about the weather. Finally, the man said, "Are you Eddie Reinhardt's dad?"

"Yes, I am," I replied. "Did you know Eddie?"

"Yes!" He answered. "Let me tell you about your son. I've been around this school a long time and watched lots of kids come and go over the years, but your son was one of the few who ever paid me any attention. Anytime we passed in the hallway, your son always had a kind word for me. I didn't forget that. I'm sorry he was hurt and I hope he gets better. Give him my best."

"At age 19, Ed was more complete as an individual than most people ever become," said his college roommate John Martin to Douglas S. Looney, writer for Sports Illustrated. "He was an excellent student and athlete. He had an incredible work ethic. He was spiritual. He had his life extremely well defined."

We all remembered his kind and gentle spirit, the kid who was always there to protect the little guy, be it a younger brother, a classmate or a co-worker. This was the type of man my son had become…and I wanted him back.

We said nothing about the outcome of his injury. He was still in critical condition and each twenty-four hour period he survived would be a milestone. Father Berg said a closing prayer and we ended our meeting with hugs and smiles.

For the first time, Pat and I decided to leave Eddie's bedside for a few hours. We needed to be away from the hospital and alone with the other children.

We went to the Oregon coast that afternoon. We pulled off the highway just below the lighthouse in Devil's Head State Park. In the cove just below the lighthouse, we walked the beach. I walked along with my hands in my pockets looking at the sand and rocks. The tremendous roar of the waves crashing on the rocks only intensified my feelings of powerlessness and fear. "I'm afraid my son is dying and there is nothing I can do to save his life." Each of us walked separately and silent in our sorrow in this place of beauty.

Later, we drove to the coastal town of Florence for dinner. We would be a family again, for at least a little while. Our mood began to lighten in the little restaurant. We continued to reminisce about some of the humorous times we shared during their growing up years. The tension was broken by giddiness and laughter which seemed odd for our situation. The other patrons in the restaurant looked at us as our laughter escalated. The experience at the coast that afternoon brought us closer together and helped us through this tragedy and the uncertainties which lay ahead.

The issue of our other boys continuing to play football was heavy on my mind.

I wanted to discuss this before they headed back to school. I asked them to think about it and we would talk about it in the morning. I told them if they decided not to play again, we would certainly understand. I told them it would be better to stop playing if their hearts weren't in the game. The next morning John said, "We don't need a meeting, Dad! We're going back to our teams!" His brother Tom said, "We talked about this earlier and agreed— we want to play." As their father, I had always been on the sidelines cheering them on and if I told them now they couldn't play football, I would be a hypocrite.

That evening, the two players from the Oregon football team who had been involved in the tackle, stopped by the hospital for a visit. Between visits with Eddie, we spent the time with those two young men and our children talking about school and sports. Pat and I just listened to them talk and were happy our kids could meet them. It wasn't necessary to talk about Eddie's injury on the football field. They were two good kids, no different from our own.

We continued our vigil throughout Wednesday. The three older children went back to school and the four of us remaining with Eddie felt their absence. We established a daily routine and, anytime we both left his side, we could depend on Paul and Matthew to talk to him and read some of the hundreds of get well cards which arrived daily. We believed Eddie could hear us. We would say, "You were hurt in a football game in Oregon when your head hit the ground. We're still in Oregon. They removed a blood clot from your brain. Everyone is working to get you back to Colorado as soon as possible." Over and over we repeated variations of this speech during the day, hoping he could understand us and be less fearful.

Pat and I felt pressured by the unending number of phone calls asking us to update Eddie's condition. News media from around the country asked questions ranging from how we felt about the game of football to the medical team's use of the drug Mannitol to shrink the brain. We talked to many relatives each day keeping our families informed. Coach McCartney still wanted a report each morning about the slightest change. He advised his staff to interrupt any meeting or phone call when we called in with our report. The media were hounding him twice a day for reports for the papers and television.

The headlines on the sports page of The Denver Post before the Notre Dame game, read, "Reinhardt, not Irish, stirs McCartney." McCartney was asked by the reporter if such a tragedy had changed his outlook about football. McCartney responded, "This tragedy only reaffirmed my belief a young person must get his or her priorities in order. The rewards and returns of playing football—there is almost nothing our society offers today which can make a man out of a boy and teach wholesome values of hard work and discipline and become a member of a team."

He ended his remarks in the article by saying:

> "All the things youngsters have to learn: commitment, excellence…the very fiber of our society that's coming apart in marriages, etc. Football teaches those things. It teaches them better than anything else we have. I'm convinced of that. There isn't anything easy about playing football. It's the most difficult thing we do. It's not fun to practice; it's hard to practice. Practices are demanding. Taxing and exacting. They require all of a guy. The result is that a guy spends himself in a worthy cause and he learns to get up off the ground, time and again. He lines up, like some of my guys will, against somebody bigger, stronger and faster than they are. And you learn to compete. And battle. Eddie Reinhardt is doing that right now. He's got a great fighting heart. Football helped develop that in him. When a guy finishes playing football, regardless of how much he's played in terms of being in the limelight, he's a better man."

On Monday, nine days after the accident, a tracheotomy was performed. We were told this was standard procedure for someone in a coma this long. We signed the papers and I looked at it as one more pin for Eddie to juggle to stay alive. Word got out about this procedure and the phones started to ring.

Being out of his room was stressful for me and the phone calls were always pulling me away from Eddie's bedside. By the next morning, both monitors were reporting normal conditions, so the hospital released a medical report stating his condition had improved, but he was still on the critical list.

Nelse Hendricks was monitoring my phone calls at the office. He passed along names of clients I needed to call. In the business forms business, my competitors had been some of my best friends. I received a letter signed by five of them, volunteering to follow up on my sales calls. I gave the names of my clients to them and each worked in a different section of Denver representing Reinhardt Business Forms. Several months later at an appreciation luncheon I had for them, I reported my sales during that month were the highest they had been all year. We all enjoyed a good laugh.

Following through with my convictions of always "doing it my way," nobody else in the company was authorized to write checks. When I resigned from Control Data Corporation several years before, I told Pat, "I don't need this aggravation from management. If I can do it for them, I can start a business of my own and earn a living for us." I used to tell my boss, Joe Kane, "Don't come to Denver and harass me and my salesmen, Joe; just give me my district quota and leave me alone. I'll get the job done." Not unlike my father.

I realized then, I was the one with the problem. I've always had a problem with authority, trusting whether they were doing the right thing for me. I did not want my destiny and the welfare of my family of eight left up to someone who could fire me on a whim. I didn't want someone playing politics with my life as they worked their way into upper management. I believed I could work smarter alone and make more money. I later learned children from single parent families often grow up to become entrepreneurs.

Pat had a tough time accepting my need to start a business of our own. Trying to start a business while raising six children was more risk than she wanted to take. I assured her I could make it happen and, thanks to her faith in me and her struggle to maintain the home on a limited income, we did. We doubled our income in three years, just in time to start sending our kids to college. Even Pat finished her bachelor's degree in psychology. She needed that degree to live with me!

Finally, after two weeks away from work I decided I needed to go back to my office in Littleton and also spend some time with Tom, Paul and Matt. Two days at home were enough to pay bills and visit clients who needed my help. I spent a few minutes talking business and more time talking about Eddie. Each person I met wanted to know about his condition and when he was coming home. The newspaper printed a daily report about his condition on the cover of the sports page. I was told everyone in town was praying for him. I reported the news from home to Pat and how tough it was going to be for me to say goodbye to Paul, age 14 and Matthew, just ten.

They were frightened we might still lose Eddie and were anxious about when we would all be home again as a family. For Matthew, it seemed like an endless time of waiting with little structure in his life. I could relate to the sadness of his waiting. I just couldn't let him suffer like I had. I wanted to pick him up and bring him back to Oregon with me. Pat and I decided to do just that.

Matt was doing well in school and there was no reason for him to stay home. We convinced ourselves he would be a big help to us, talking to Eddie and reading the get well cards. Really what I was saying was I was lonesome for all the kids.

And stronger we needed to be. By Sunday evening of the second week, I was back in Eugene. By Monday morning, Dr. Hockey was sure Eddie had pneumonia. His temperature was going up, his coughing had increased and his breathing was erratic. At times, his tracheotomy tube had to be suctioned to remove mucus from his throat. This removal caused him to cough even harder and, at first, I had to leave the room because I couldn't stand to see him gag. His body would nearly sit up. Eventually, I was able to stay to hold him down throughout the procedure. The coughing spells happened every few minutes throughout the day.

Dr. Donald Hobbs, a lung specialist, was called in to review Eddie's condition. He decided Eddie needed to have tubes inserted in each side of his chest to drain the fluid which was building up. The worst of all sights I experienced throughout his recovery was after surgery, when they placed him on a special bed. It was designed in the shape of a cross with his body strapped onto a horizontal frame and his arms stretched out and secured with clamps. A machine turned the bed and his body from side to side. It took 45 seconds to turn from left vertical back to right vertical. Each time his body nearly fell out of the bed as he reached the vertical point. At the vertical point, I would run around the bed and steady his head. Forty five seconds later, I would run around to the other side. Hour after hour we stayed by his side.

All the monitors were attached, along with the two new chest tubes. The beeping and the drawing of lines across the screens continued.

"This is so pitiful," I screamed inside. "So many things to juggle, papers to sign and this damn squeaky machine keeps turning Eddie over and over. He isn't going to make it!"

He was three years old when we first rushed him to an emergency room. A dose of penicillin caused his face and neck to swell and we were told he was allergic to penicillin at that time. Pat explained giving penicillin could cause a reaction called anaphylactic shock which could cause immediate death. From then on, the doctors had treated him for minor conditions with different antibiotics. Soon after his injury, we reported this information to the medical staff for their records.

Tuesday afternoon, 17 days after the accident, Dr. Hobbs approached Pat and me to discuss Eddie's condition. He again asked what we remembered about Eddie's reaction to penicillin when he was little. He said, "If we don't see some change by morning, we will have to give him penicillin. We can't wait any longer. If he does have a reaction from the penicillin, we will be ready with a treatment for that. We're running out of time and this is our last chance to save his life. We will wait until morning."

The fear he would die was constantly on my mind and I became quiet and withdrawn. I couldn't resign myself to believe he was dying nor could I feel any hope he would live. I thought about all the people who had told us during the past two weeks they believed he would survive. "All the pins are in the air and we're juggling as fast as we can." I thought. "There's nothing more to do but pray."

Heaven Can Wait

*F*or me, each day was becoming a bigger tragedy than the day before. The moment I woke up, I felt the knife twisting inside me as I agonized about what Eddie was going through. I was so tired from the stress and worry, I was exhausted each night and quickly fell asleep. The mornings however were difficult to face and this particular morning was the worst because of the increased possibility of losing Eddie.

By the time we got to the hospital, I could feel the tension building in intensive care and I thought I also detected an unusual distance from the medical staff. People who were often friendly and jovial, were now describing the past night in a serious tone. It was as if they were holding back their usual loving attitude toward Eddie to protect themselves from the heartache of losing a friend. They had given everything to save his life and, now, that friendship might end.

Dr. Hobbs met us in the waiting room and explained Eddie's pneumonia continued to worsen. He said, in spite of Eddie's history of allergic reaction, he must give the penicillin as soon as possible. I was cautious about trusting the decision of his physicians.

Pat, in her spirituality, had decided to leave him in the hands of Jesus. "If Jesus wants Eddie home with Him, I would freely give him up," she said.

I couldn't give him up that easily. I could barely think about losing him now. Again, I would be left behind by someone I loved so much. The possibility of losing him kept reminding me of saying goodbye to my dad and watching him too, leave me.

It was about this time a staff member approached us with an organ donor card.

"Mr. and Mrs. Reinhardt, it is very difficult to say this." Slowly she went on. "We want to offer you the possibility of donating Ed's organs. I know this is not easy for your to hear."

If there was any way our hearts could become heavier, they undoubtedly were now. The thin thread of hope we were clinging to, was unraveling further.

"We will need some time to talk and decide," I responded hesitantly. The response was compassionate.

"We do not need an answer right away. We will not need an answer until later and only if the penicillin isn't helping him and his condition worsens."

There was no initial reaction to a small dose of penicillin so by ten o'clock a large dose was administered. He was given as much of the antibiotic in one dose as one normally would take in a week.

Sacred Heart Hospital is located right across the street from the University of Oregon campus. After lunch, Pat and I went for a walk around campus to talk about our decision of whether to donate Eddie's organs. Students of Eddie's age were everywhere. Some were throwing Frisbees or laughing and talking to their friends. The dread we felt contrasted sharply with the normalcy of their lives.

Pat broke our silence, "You know he would give everything. In fact, we both know what he would choose. We have to consider his willingness to give all of himself to someone else."

That was simple for me to understand, but my own selfishness told me "No! He has already given enough." I was torn knowing his voice in this decision would say to let go and let him help someone else. I didn't know who to listen to. Eddie's silent voice spoke to me the loudest and had we been forced to make that decision, I would have agreed to donate his organs.

This was a time I saw my wife at her best as a person and as a mother. Her faith never wavered. She was able to give up Eddie if that was what was asked of her. Her faith in God reminded me of the Bible story about Abraham trusting God when asked to give up his son, Isaac. It was harder for me. I remembered walking around this same college campus 32 years earlier, pondering the thought of losing my dad through divorce. Now, I was pondering the possibility of giving up my son. "I can't lose again," I thought.

They continued the penicillin throughout the day without any signs of an adverse reaction. This treatment was our last hope as we waited during the afternoon and early evening for some response. There was none. I was still fighting an internal battle about donating Eddie's organs. I could hardly say a word to Pat without crying. I told her I had to get out of the hospital and go for a walk. I had to sort this out alone.

I barely made it down the elevator and through the lobby. My stomach was in knots and my throat was raw from holding back the sobbing. Out on the sidewalk and finally alone, I bent over by a tree and grabbed my stomach. I let myself cry out over the real possibility of losing my son. I thought of him struggling to suck in every drop of oxygen he could. I was losing control in every area of life and it was only a matter of time before I lost Eddie. I began walking down the street, stumbling at times. I passed people and I looked away.

In my aimless walk I was drawn back to places where I had said goodbye to my father. Throughout my life, those places were frequently on my mind and often made me feel depressed.

The bus station was the same. The neon sign of a Greyhound dog was still racing across the window. It was closed and, as I stood there looking at my reflection in the darkened window, a police car drove by slowly. The courthouse had moved to new facilities, although the building was still there in the middle of the city. I could still remember the heavily decorated dark wood of the courtroom. I wondered what had taken its place. I recalled the kindness of the judge in contrast to Dad's evil accusation about Mom's refusal to move to Oregon. I heard the judge bang the gavel and say, "Divorce granted."

I walked a few blocks to the railroad station. Amtrak was using the facility now, with daily passenger trips from Portland to San Francisco. I sat on the bench outside the entrance and couldn't remember ever being inside the station or boarding the train. My brother Jim still swears I was in a daze after the trial right up until we reached Klamath Falls, Oregon, the next afternoon.

By now, I could go into the Eugene Hotel without sobbing. It was no longer a hotel but a residential apartment building for senior citizens. I wandered into the lobby and was greeted by an older lady, curious as to why I was there at nearly midnight. I told her I had stayed in the hotel many years before and I was staying in town again because my son had been injured playing football. She had heard of my son's injury and expressed her sympathy. Hardly anything in the lobby had changed. I would like to have gone up to the sixth floor to look out over the city to see "UO" outlined in white painted rocks on the hillside.

It was past midnight and I still wanted to visit the former ice cream shop on the corner of Broadway and Pearl, where I said goodbye to Dad on that cold and rainy February afternoon 32 years ago. It was now an upscale café called Zenon. I stayed there a long time, thinking about my frivolous conversation with Dad to stall for time as we said goodbye.

The police car passed a second time, prompting me to keep moving. I crossed the street just as I had done years before with Mom and Jim and, halfway across, I turned and looked back. There was nobody. I was the only person on the street. As I walked along, I was somewhat relieved of the heavy burden I felt when I left the hospital. Slowly, a peacefulness came over me and I reached out easily toward God. "Lord, will Eddie live?"

Gradually, as I walked and listened, an idea unfolded which showed me what I believed was my answer.

"A long time ago, I brought you home from Oregon and, whether you know it or not, I have been caring for you and protecting you. You have had a good life with a fine family and

I have provided for all your needs. A few years ago, I brought your father home from Oregon, just as you asked. I did not forget your prayers. Eddie will get well and he, too, will come home."

At that moment I understood God had been caring for me all along. He had answered my prayer and brought Dad home. Even now, I could sense God working in the intensive care unit to save my son. I seldom know if I'm hearing answers from the Lord or if it's my imagination. I have to rely on the change His word begins to make in my life to be sure I can trust what I heard is of the Lord.

Still several blocks from the hospital, I began to feel the joy of believing Eddie was going to survive.

"I have to get back to the hospital and tell Pat," I thought. I felt such a lightness, I wanted to run and kick my feet. Fortunately, before I took my first leap, I noticed the same police officer drive by more slowly and look more closely at me. I constrained my emotions and moved on.

It was two in the morning when I arrived back at the hospital. I could barely wait to find Pat to tell her I believed Eddie was going to live. I found her in the waiting room and sat down beside her.

I asked, "How's Eddie?"

She had the most hopeful expression I'd seen in several days. She said, "His temperature has been dropping and his coughing has slowed down some." As I reached out to squeeze her hand, I said, "He's going to make it, Pat. Eddie's going to live."

A New Beginning

*J*n the days which followed our hopes for Eddie's survival grew stronger. Dr. Hockey was sounding more optimistic. The nurses reported Eddie was moving his left arm and once lifted it up to his chest as if he were reaching for his neck, maybe to pull out his tracheotomy tube. The doctor explained this was a good sign and he might be coming out of the coma. Pat and I grasped at any good news.

Over breakfast a few days later, I was able to relate to Pat the experience of my midnight walk through Eugene. Pat also had an experience that night which encouraged us both. While praying with her hands over Eddie's head, she realized his swollen brain was herniated out of the large hole in his skull. In sheer horror she ran from the room and called Father Timothy Berg. He met her in his office. She explained part of Eddie's brain was outside of his skull.

"Is this a new occurrence?" he asked

"No" Pat answered, "I'm sure it's been this way since the first surgery three weeks ago."

Father Berg replied, "Then this isn't something new, it's something you've just discovered."

Even though his logic somewhat calmed her, she introduced another frightening thought. "They say it will be a miracle if he survives."

Father Berg paused for a moment, then looking directly into her eyes said softly, "We have miracles here."

Eddie was now in the seventeenth day of his coma. We heard it said a coma can be beneficial while the brain is healing. Conversely, we were also told the longer the coma continued, the more damage could be expected to his brain.

We speculated, "Can he hear us? Is he aware of what is happening and, most importantly, when will he wake up?" The Hollywood version of coming out of a coma is usually nothing like the real thing. In the movies, a light switch turns on and the person wakes up and says, "Hi, Mom and Dad!" Eddie's return from the coma would be very gradual.

A few nights later I had a dream which seemed to address some of our concerns. In my dream I was leaning against the car watching Eddie play basketball with a friend in our driveway. Eddie was very competitive and always played enthusiastically, even against his own brothers. Eddie and his friend were playing so hard, sweat was pouring down their faces. His opponent was causing Eddie to play some tough basketball, but at the same time, I could sense their unwavering friendship and respect for one another. His partner had a full beard and long dark hair. He was about 6 ½-inches shorter than Eddie but made up for the height difference by speed and accurate shooting.

As I looked closely at him, I realized this player was Jesus. I wasn't shocked at seeing them play because Eddie had always had a real relationship with the Lord. Since that dream when I think about Eddie's coma, I first see the picture of Eddie and Jesus playing an aggressive game of basketball.

There was one other scene. A split-rail fence stood between where I was leaning against the car and where Jesus and Eddie were playing. In the dream a feeling of loneliness went through me when I realized I was separated from Jesus. Something was keeping me away.

I decided to make a second trip back to Denver. I had to see some clients and I needed to visit the University of Colorado Athletic Department to talk about our insurance policies and determine who was the primary carrier for Eddie's accident.

Eventually, we determined $3.5 million was available. It was just as Coach McCartney had said during his recruiting visit in our living room: "All medical costs would be paid by the university football program." The total cost eventually reached a half million dollars.

I arrived home on Wednesday morning, going to see my clients and then visiting insurance people in the athletic department. I stopped in to see Coach McCartney and explained the progress Eddie was making and how excited we were just to see him moving again. He asked me if I would stop by the locker room before practice and tell the players how their teammate was doing.

I thought, "I've never heard of anyone being asked to address a college football team except the coach." I questioned whether I had the courage to stand in front of them and explain what was happening to Eddie. I was reluctant to describe his bout with pneumonia and how he nearly died. I still questioned my own belief Eddie would survive. Again, I had to remind myself how so many people in Eugene came to tell us they believed he would recover.

"Yes I will, Coach. I'd be honored to talk to the team about Eddie." When I met with the team later that afternoon, I said, "As sure as I'm standing here, I believe Eddie is getting better." The team was very quiet and attentive to what I had to say. "We nearly lost him from pneumonia last week. He had a high temperature and fluid was collecting in his lungs. They installed tubes in either side of his chest to drain his lungs. Finally, he was given as much penicillin in a day as you would normally take in a week. After a few days he rallied and his body is fighting back. We stay with him all day and late into the night. Nothing has been said about when he will be moved back to Denver. He is still in a coma. Many people are praying for him. I know many of you pray and I want to ask you to please keep on praying because he has a long way to go. Someday." I said, "Eddie will be here to cheer you on to victory." I promised them I'd do everything I could to make that happen.

After being home a few days, everything happening in Oregon seemed like a bad dream. I vacillated between wanting to stay in Denver and wanting to rush back to Eddie's side.

I attended Paul's Thursday afternoon football game and we all stopped at McDonald's for supper, just like old times. Paul, Matt and I attended Tom's Friday night football game. I felt normal being in the stands with parents of the other players. Nevertheless, all the time my mind was with Eddie and what was happening to him so far away. Yet I reminded myself we had five other children who needed my attention.

By Sunday evening, 22 days since the accident, I was back at Eddie's bedside. For the next five days we arrived at the hospital early and did not leave until after 10 P.M. One of us was always with Eddie. On Friday, the morning of the 26th day, Dr. Hockey announced during his morning rounds, "I think Eddie will be well enough to travel back to Colorado; that is, if he continues to improve as he has been during the past week. I believe his pneumonia is under control and his lungs are improving. We can start making arrangements for a medical evacuation plane out of the University of Washington to take Eddie home on Monday, October 15th."

At one point, Dr. Hockey asked if some of Eddie's friends could come to Oregon for a visit. In spite of the sacrifice of time and money, they were quick to respond. First it was Rob Semin and Tiffany Hill. Tiffany played basketball for Colorado and was the only female who would challenge Eddie in playing one-on-one basketball. Rob and Ed were on the same basketball team in high school and had been good friends for years. Both of them did everything they could to wake him up. Rob shouted "Hey Rhino," and Tiffany cranked up the rock music tapes she brought along.

The second team of visitors was John Martin and Regina Regnvall. John was Ed's college roommate and Regina, a friend from high school. Their approach was gentler, but so loving. Despite their efforts, Eddie slept on.

Another welcomed visitor was my older brother John from Wisconsin. He stayed overnight at the hospital with Eddie when

I took my second trip back to Denver. His concern for Eddie brought our relationship closer.

At last, arrangements were being made for Eddie to be transferred to the University of Colorado Health Sciences Center in Denver. He was on a respirator and monitors were still communicating his status with beeps and white lines. Dr. Kindt, the director of neurosurgery at the CU Health Sciences Center, would be traveling back to Oregon again, this time to accompany Eddie during the plane trip home. He would be assisted by two nurses. Because I was going with them, the trip was delayed by one day because the plane with an extra seat for me wasn't available until Tuesday, October 16.

Although Pat and I were disappointed at the delay, we insisted I be on that plane. I wanted to be with him just as I wanted to bring Dad home from Oregon. Later I realized the delay by one day brought the number of days Eddie was in Oregon to 42—the same number of years Dad had lived in this state he called, "God's country."

Standing over Eddie's bed on the eve of our departure, I said, "Just one more night before we go home, Eddie." I repeated this over and over, hoping he would hear me as we watched the Denver Broncos play the Green Bay Packers on Monday Night Football. They played during one of the worst snowstorms the Denver Broncos had ever played in. I had never seen a game with so much slipping , sliding, fumbling and incomplete passing.

After the game, the television reporters presented weather reports and announced the airport in Denver would be closed after midnight. Our plan to leave early the next morning and be in Denver by noon was delayed. Now we would leave Eugene at one in the afternoon, weather permitting.

The next morning I watched the medical team prepare for the move. It reminded me of the countdown to launch a rocket as many procedures had to be followed. For instance, Eddie couldn't be given tube feedings for six hours before flight time to prevent nausea during the trip. So, between the weather and his feeding routine, the intensive care staff was working diligently to stay on schedule. I just stood around watching them and drinking lots of coffee.

All last-minute preparations were made for my son to be taken down the elevator to the ambulance. The hospital respirator and monitors had to be disconnected from their power and reconnected to portable hand-operated machines. The monitors never missed a beep during the procedures. "Nothing is going to happen to this guy now," a nurse remarked. "He's come too far to have any more problems."

I had been standing in the midst of the activity when I was paged to the telephone. I thought it might be Pat so I accepted the call, only to hear a voice say, "I'm John McGrath, a rookie reporter for The Denver Post. You know, I'm a new kid on the block and I want to ask you some questions about your trip home and about Saturday's upcoming game in Boulder between Colorado and Nebraska. Your son John is playing for Nebraska and will be playing against Eddie's team. What do you think of that?" I was stunned—first, to be put on the spot to answer questions about Eddie and, second, to be relating my feelings about the game on Saturday between two teams who had meant so much to me.

"Two years! Two years I've waited for this game. Now I can't do anything to change the circumstances," I said, "although I do wish there was a way to hold off playing this game until another time. John and Ed had wanted to play this game together."

"For me, It would have been the greatest game of their careers. I watched them grow up playing sports, through grade school and high school, and now they are playing against each other in college. It reminds me of the war between the States where brother fought against brother, only now one of the brothers is wounded and fighting for his life."

I answered question after question with whatever words came to mind. It all seemed so unimportant to me considering what I was watching down the hall. I explained what was going on and I'd have to leave when Eddie's entourage reached the elevator. I continued pouring out my feelings while at the same time wishing he would stop asking questions. When they motioned for me to leave with them, I told him I must go and hung up the receiver. As I walked down the hall, I felt sick inside from talking to the reporter. "God only knows what he will write," I thought.

I really didn't want to think about the Saturday game because only one son would be playing and there wasn't a damn thing I could do to postpone that event.

A Promise
to Return

*J*t was raining in Eugene as we drove through town to the airport. It reminded me of leaving Eugene 32 years earlier. People were walking peacefully, minding their business just as before, and I was—just as before—a person in crisis.

I thought about all that had happened in what seemed like such a short time. It was awkward riding in the back of an ambulance, something I had never done. As we passed over the Willamette River I glanced back at Sacred Heart Hospital and the bright red sign which read, "EUGENE HOTEL."

I thought about all the new people I had met over the past 32 days and how our lives were drawn together by Eddie's accident. I thought about the hundreds of conversations I had, all centered around how to help him survive. Throughout all this, I was thinking about my own loss while no one but Pat knew anything about my parents' divorce here.

I had to admit, the negative attitude I developed from being here 32 yars earlier, never gave me the kind of peace that I had just experienced, from working with so many kind people. Working closely with others had helped me understand just how dependent we are on each other. I finally was beginning to realize no one is an island.

I was becoming painfully aware of my failures. How much time had I wasted using my skillful techniques to isolate and protect myself? Did people see through me as I attempted to prove I was just as good as anyone else? Had I known my philosophy was so distorted, I wouldn't have encouraged my kids to compete so hard in everything they did; not just to win, but to protect themselves from ever getting hurt by losing. Teaching them to compete was a good thing to do, but I encouraged their competition for the wrong reason.

As we got farther away, I felt uneasy about taking Eddie from the security of the hospital. I felt helpless around the competent medical people who now had my son's life in their hands. I was forced to learn to trust others. I also had to trust the Lord, believing He was working through others to bring Eddie home.

Some of the hospital nurses accompanied us to the airport. Saying goodbye to them was the hardest part of the trip. We had grown close under stressful conditions and it seemed awkward to end our relationship so abruptly. Goodbye didn't seem to be enough. To ease the pain of our departure, I renewed my promise, someday I would return with Eddie to have him meet them and thank them himself for working so hard to save his life.

I pictured coming to Eugene with Eddie. We would retrace our steps through Sacred Heart Hospital and walk the football field to the 37-yard-line where he fell and where his whole life changed forever. Maybe he would need to go back to that very place to pick himself up and start over.

On board the plane, it took only a few minutes before we broke into the sunshine above Eugene. The sunny sky was a relief after the damp, cloudy morning below and it helped to lift a heavy burden from my shoulders. I took a deep breath, settled back and began listening to the pilots who were talking to flight controllers on the ground.

I watched Dr. Kindt and the nurses work with Eddie. They still had to suction his throat through the tracheotomy tube. The nurses hand-pumped the respirator. Monitors registered blood pressure, heart rate, pulse and body temperature.

Sitting near his feet, I decided my job was to continually tell Eddie what was happening. I reminded him he had been hurt in a football game and had suffered a brain injury in Oregon. I told him we would be back in Denver in a few hours and he would be seeing lots of his friends.

I asked the pilot questions about the plane and asked Dr. Kindt simple questions about what medical procedures would follow after we returned to Denver. He talked about further tests and the possibility of installing a shunt to drain the fluid from the ventricles in Eddie's brain. His swollen brain prevented the doctor from closing his skull. Part of his brain protruded through a circular opening, covered only by skin and dressings. Dr. Kindt believed we would see Eddie being more responsive after they implanted a shunt.

The aircraft was small and crowded. The body of the plane was barely six feet wide, leaving room only for Eddie lying on the stretcher on one side and a bench attached to the other side for seating for the medical team.

There was no aisle. The medical team's arms and hands were constantly in motion and occasionally one hand would reach for a sip from a can of soda pop. The technicians shared a cooler of soft drinks with me and Dr. Kindt and, by the time we reached the halfway point, I was sitting back, finally relaxed, reading Sports Illustrated and drinking my second can of Pepsi.

I kept thinking about the busy morning, especially about the telephone interview with John McGrath from The Denver Post. I wondered what he was going to say about us. After my second can of Pepsi my eyes discreetly searched the small plane for a bathroom only to realize there wasn't one. As the trip progressed I became increasingly jealous of the catheter bag suspended beneath Eddie's bed.

Making a
Promise to Eddie

As soon as he arrived at the hospital in Denver, doctors initiated a complete medical examination and I was told Eddie would not return to the intensive care area until after nine P.M. I was able to go home to see Tom, Paul and Matt and their maternal grandparents who had been caring for them for over a month. It was wonderful to hug the boys and know I didn't have to leave them again. Because of the snowstorm, many flights had been canceled delaying Pat's arrival back home from Eugene. At home I learned she was finally able to get a flight out of Portland.

When the doctors finished their evaluation later that evening, they explained to me Eddie was still very sick and his condition would be listed as serious. They believed the pneumonia was under control but because of a build-up of brain fluid, there was no sign of his regaining consciousness.

The CAT scan showed there was a large amount of fluid in the center of his brain. Dr. Kindt explained how the ventricles which normally drained the excess fluids from his head were not working properly. He suggested a permanent shunt be installed to help with this. He believed there would be little improvement until this procedure was done. We agreed and I signed the papers authorizing this operation. They would also

146

do an angiogram to see whether there was evidence of a blood clot or an aneurysm.

The doctor finished his report and left me alone with Eddie with much to think about. Eddie's tall, once muscular body had lost nearly 75 pounds. His weight had dropped from 235 to 161 pounds. His face appeared thin and gaunt. His hair, shaved for two previous operations, was two different lengths and his head remained bandaged. He was very weak and barely moved his arms and legs.

His eyes were open and seemed to look around the room. I wondered if he recognized me. I continued talking to him and sometimes played his music, hoping there would be some breakthrough. I longed for anything to tell me he was back and yet I feared what he would be when he woke up. Would he be as I knew him, or would there be so much damage he could not function as before?

More importantly, would I be able to deal with the outcome? Would I have the courage to stay or would I run? How much of my life would be asked of me and how much would I be willing to give? I remembered Coach Bill McCartney saying he had seen many injuries, though none like this, during his football coaching career.

I sat there quietly holding Eddie's hand and occasionally rubbing his shoulders, still the only place on his chest where I could lay my hand. I assured him I was with him and told him we were back in Colorado and he was doing well. The respirator and the monitors kept their pace and sometimes picked up a rhythm which sounded like the beat of music, singing out, telling me Eddie was just going to keep on getting better.

I began to think about all that had happened during the past month and I started asking myself again, "Why in Eugene, Lord?" I hadn't had the terrible physical damage Eddie had, but what happened to me as a result of a divorce certainly caused many changes in my life. The effects of divorce aren't physical, but they do make a difference in the way a person lives and thinks throughout his lifetime.

At that moment I spoke out loud to my son. "Eddie, I promise you I will do everything possible to bring you back from your injury. I will never leave you. I love you, Eddie." Then I prayed, "Lord, help me keep my promise."

I was alone with Eddie until well after midnight when I decided I needed to go to bed. I went upstairs to a room designated for us by the hospital and got ready for bed. I lay there thinking back over this very long day and felt some sense of optimism the shunt to be installed by Dr. Kindt might end the coma.

Just before I drifted off to sleep I remembered another night in a hospital nearly 40 years before, right after my dad had gone away. I was nearly ten and told I was to have my tonsils and adenoids removed. I woke up after the operation and saw my mom standing beside the bed. Some of my pain was in my nose and throat where I expected it to be. However, I was trying to understand why I was feeling another discomfort below my waist. Barely able to talk, I gestured to my mother to ask why it was hurting "down there."

With some hesitation and much embarrassment, since she always avoided any questions about sex, she finally blurted out I had been circumcised. That's how I learned what circumcision was all about. For years, I teased her about my adenoids being located below my belt, whereas the adenoids of my friends were located near their nose.

I thought about my promises to Eddie to stay with him and to bring him back and never to stop trying to help him. I thought about my telling him I loved him. It seemed strange to me in those two short months I had, for the first time, told two men I loved them: first my dad, then my own son. Before falling asleep, the last thing I remembered was feeling good about myself. Maybe it was the beginning of finally loving myself.

By six in the morning I was back in Eddie's room and I learned his night had been restful with less coughing. The nurses continued suctioning the tracheotomy, a procedure which still caused me to retch and gag. Maybe his coma was a blessing for him because of the torment he would suffer if he were conscious.

I thought about the days and months ahead. More and more I realized the end was nowhere in sight and my heart ached because I couldn't do more to help my son. I gritted my teeth and renewed my promise of the night before.

The orderlies arrived about 8:30 to take him away for further tests and said he would be gone for a couple of hours. Pat and I and her parents had planned to meet for breakfast in the hospital cafeteria and, when I arrived there, Pat asked whether I had read the morning paper. She opened it up, and there on the front page of the sports section was the article written by the "rookie" John McGrath, about the Colorado-Nebraska football game entitled "The Game Won't Wait for the Reinhardts." As I sat there reading with tears dripping on the newspaper, this rookie reporter from The Denver Post had touched on every emotion I felt about the game.

"If the world were just, or if football schedules had a heart, Colorado and Nebraska would put off playing Saturday afternoon at Folsom Field. "Go home," kind and wise old men would say at each turnstile. "Please."

If the world were just and if football schedules had a heart, Colorado and Nebraska would meet when, and only when Pat and Ed Reinhardt Sr. could sit in the stands and watch their boys trot onto the field from opposite sidelines: John Reinhardt from Nebraska's and Ed Reinhardt Jr. from Colorado's.

When they could watch their boys marching to the beat of a different bass drummer and feel—indeed revel—in a peculiar joy afterward; it mattered not which team won, but that two young men, as brothers, had been able to square off on each's own terms, as opponents.

It's as if John, a senior, and Ed Jr., a sophomore, saw the same destination and decided upon different avenues. They were aligned in spirit, yet independent in procedure: Brothers.

And so it is amid this profound human dilemma the schedule, impervious and impersonal to the end, decrees, "Kickoff!"

Pat and I both watched the game that afternoon in Boulder. We watched our son John play against Colorado with the same intensity he'd always had to win, just as I had advised him to do the night before. If Eddie had been able, he too would have told John this was not the time to let up, but to play his damnedest to win for his Nebraska Cornhuskers, just like Eddie would have done to win for his Colorado Buffaloes, if only he could.

During the weeks to follow, and prior to his weekly coaches TV show on Sunday evenings, Coach McCartney stopped by the hospital to visit and pray for Eddie. Coach McCartney always wanted to have the latest medical update to report to the fans when he was questioned. I looked forward to his visits because he always prayed over Eddie and for me and my family. His encouraging words helped me get through the week.

During one of his visits, he asked me whether our two younger boys, Paul and Matt, would like to be ball boys during the Colorado-Oklahoma game. I responded they would like that and I would enjoy taking them. Nevertheless, I felt a tightening in my stomach as I thought about watching another game played without Eddie. I knew it would only get tougher for me the next time if I turned down this offer and I didn't want to start running away from situations which reminded me of Eddie's loss.

We arrived at the stadium early enough to get them settled on the sidelines and to learn their assignments. It was a cold, cloudy November kind of day in Boulder, now over two months since the accident, and being alone I couldn't have felt more depressed. I hesitated to go inside and just sit, so I decided to walk around the stadium to get rid of some tension and to keep warm. As I walked by each gate, I was shocked to see college students working at booths selling candy under signs saying, Help the Reinhardt Family.

Gate after gate, kids called out to ask people for donations. I choked up and rushed back to my gate to go inside. I stopped just before entering for one more look so I could grasp what was really happening. I leaned against a tree and pulled my ski mask down until my face was covered because tears were streaming down my cheeks.

My first impulse was to run from the truth, that those kids were begging people to help the Reinhardts. In spite of my reaction, though, I found it strangely consoling to see a lady from

Oklahoma donate ten dollars and to hear her say, "I have read the papers, and what a fine young man Eddie must be. He certainly deserves our prayers."

Still, it seemed their helping Eddie was a reflection on my inability to provide for my family. Even if our names had been different it might have helped me to understand and accept their kindness was meant for Eddie and not for me.

Just before the game began, they announced there would be a moment of silence for the fallen CU player, Eddie Reinhardt. The announcement filled me with sadness. I realized how alone I felt in the midst of nearly 50,000 people. The afternoon proceeded downhill from the starting whistle. Colorado was getting beat up on every play.

I'm sure the fellow next to me thought I was acting strangely and I was. I seldom cheered and frequently wiped the tears from my eyes as I was constantly thinking about Eddie. I was also thinking about the fundraiser outside, so I stayed in my seat during halftime.

I kept telling myself I didn't need their help and I could take care of Eddie and my family myself. "Who am I if my work doesn't make me somebody?" I thought. "What other purpose is there for my life if it isn't providing for my family?"

My thoughts had me trembling and crying so much I couldn't even see the game. Through the first three quarters I felt truly defeated. I sat there freezing cold and feeling miserable, repeating over and over to myself I wouldn't care anymore and I couldn't hold on any longer.

Then, early in the fourth quarter, I began to feel some relief from my misery. I didn't notice the cold and, in fact, I seemed to be warm and comfortable. It seemed as if a concept was being revealed to me. It was not like the voice which had been driving me for so many years to turn away from people. Instead, the sense was of letting go, of letting people help me. "You can't stand behind those walls any longer. You're not alone." A peacefulness came over me, the same kind of peace I felt after my long walk around Eugene when I first started believing Eddie was going to live.

Suddenly I noticed people were leaving and I realized the game had ended. The score was Oklahoma 42 and Colorado 17. Colorado ended the season with only one win the entire season. Colorado had suffered another defeat but the peaceful feelings and warmth stayed with me as I walked out of the stadium. For the first time in a long time, it felt good to walk shoulder to shoulder among the crowd. I realized we are all just people, working, struggling, laughing, crying—all with our problems and all with our capacity to love and help one another. That day I realized just how good people really are and how much God must love them for wanting to help the Reinhardts.

Awakening

*T*he days that followed the move to Colorado demanded a lot of energy from Pat and me as we tried to adjust to a different hospital. The University of Colorado Health Sciences Center was much larger than Sacred Heart Hospital in Eugene. There were new people and new routines and Eddie was frequently checked by medical students making patient rounds with their instructors. We objected to their talking over his bed about his condition. Finally, we had to insist any conversations about his condition be conducted away from his bedside. They seemed to take offense at this affront to their developing medical egos, but we were learning, too. In Oregon we learned to be more in charge of Eddie's care and decided we would insist on certain considerations for Eddie here at home.

After he was moved out of intensive care and into a private room we soon realized how isolated he was from the nursing staff. In intensive care, the nurses were only a few feet away. Now, we discovered, unless someone looked in on him he could be alone for hours. He couldn't even ring a call bell. Pat was staying with him all day and I was coming in at 5 p.m. staying until after 10:30. Recognizing his need for someone to stay with him all night, we approached the head nurse. She told us the hospital did not provide private nurses. She explained Eddie would be all right just having an aide look in on him occasionally. This didn't comfort us, so we tried to solve the problem ourselves.

We took turns staying the first three nights and realized we couldn't keep up the pace, so some generous friends agreed to stay the night with him. On one of those nights, Dr. Kindt, Eddie's neurosurgeon, suggested we go to a nearby theater and see a movie about Mozart, called *"Amadeus."*

It was a sad movie about Mozart's hardships and finally his death. We felt more tired and depressed after the movie and, on the way home, talked about Mozart being a perfectionist surrounded by mediocrity. Somehow, this movie caused us to rally to fight for our belief Eddie needed the best care possible and it was our job to see he got it without compromise. By morning we were knocking on the door of the patient relations representative, insisting Eddie have a nurse. Eddie got a nurse.

As a result of all Pat and I had been through during the previous six weeks, we learned some new ways of working together. We agreed to first come together in prayer and give the decision to the Lord and then trust Him to help us make the right choices.

In addition, when we were asked to make any sort of judgment, we would reflect on it for two or three days to determine whether we had any doubts or needed more information.

Little did we realize what good this method was doing for our relationship and how it was bringing us together. At no time during this family tragedy did we accuse each other or cast blame on the other for this terrible thing that had happened to Eddie. Instead, we became closer and stronger in our ability to work together. The suffering we had been through had brought us closer and made us more respectful of one another.

After the shunt surgery, Dr. Kindt reported the swelling was going down and he would expect a lot more movement and awareness from Eddie once the fluid level was normal. Such changes meant there would be a better chance for Eddie to regain consciousness. The shunt was doing its job, so they performed the final surgery to close the opening in his skull with an acrylic plastic. The juggler could now retire another of the pins he had been tossing. Now that Eddie was closer to consciousness, it appeared his juggling act would soon be finished.

The anxiety began to build in all of us as we talked about how close he was to waking. "What will be the first signs?" we wondered. Would he just look up at us and say, "Hi, Mom?" Or would he emerge from his quiet place very subtly. Would he be like he was before the accident? The time was nearing for us to find out.

Eddie was honored by an endless stream of visitors. They were college and high school friends, parents of his friends and neighbors. Father Fred McCallin, pastor of St. Thomas More parish, visited weekly as did Father Bob DeRouen, S.J., a family friend who taught at Regis College. Coach Bill McCartney continued his weekly Sunday visits during the remainder of the football season. Eddie's bed was raised to a partial sitting position and he was looking around as if he were awake, but he showed no reaction to anything said or done around his bed. At first his friends felt awkward about being with him. Often they were near tears. I could sense their frustration and realized I needed to monitor their visits by meeting them at the door to explain how to approach him. I suggested they had to do all the talking and they might start out by telling a story or anecdote about a time they had shared together. This approach could help stimulate his long-term memory. I also suggested they tell him funny stories since humor is a high level of brain function. Fortunately, there was no shortage of wisecrackers among his friends.

We saw gradual improvement each day. He seemed so close and we were so desperate and anxious to have him back. He had been away from us for 60 days and we were growing weary, waiting and searching for some sign of his return. Eddie's coma reminded me of waiting for my dad to come home.

One evening I was sitting in Eddie's room reading the newspaper. A friend of his from high school, Ken Dickson, was recounting a story about the time Eddie tried to con the bus driver into letting him drive the school bus. Evidently Eddie had tried several schemes. Finally, the driver said he would let him drive the bus only if Eddie fixed him up with a certain pretty girl from school. Eddie would never dare drive the bus, but he couldn't pass up the opportunity to see how far the driver would go.

I had been reading and listening at the same time and, when the story concluded, I heard what sounded like a chuckle. I didn't recognize the sound but I turned around and saw Eddie's slight smile. Then I heard the sound again. I ran over to his bed, grabbed him, and said, "That's it, that's it! You're back!" Eddie looked at me like, "What's the big deal?" I asked his friend to tell him another story or say something funny. "Do anything to make him smile," I said.

I called home to tell Pat and the family, and they were all overjoyed to hear the news. Then I ran down the hall and told the nurse at the nurses' station but found them unimpressed. I didn't care. I wanted to shout for joy. I couldn't wait for the doctor's visit to show him what was happening; but like a child asked to show off for grandma, Eddie clammed up and drifted back into his coma when the doctor arrived.

The doctor indicated Eddie's response needed to be in the doctor's presence before he could declare the coma had ended. I realized the doctor wasn't going to get too excited either, but *I* wanted to open the windows on the sixth floor and shout this wonderful news to the world.

His friend ended his visit about nine and again I was alone with Eddie. I turned off his music and sat there by his side. I was sure he could hear me now, and I needed to talk and explain to him the whole story of why he was in the hospital. We had shared the story with him many times but we were never sure he heard us. This time I went through the accident step by step.

I explained his surgeries, and how he almost died of pneumonia. I read some of the cards from people around the country who were praying for him and telling him he would recover. Finally, I was able to tell him how lonely I was without him and how much he meant to me as my son and how happy I was to have him back home.

As his awareness slowly improved, he was able to respond to the doctor's commands and after 62 days, they declared him out of the coma. Arrangements were then made to move him to Craig Hospital in Englewood, about five miles from our home in Littleton. This hospital is nationally known for work with spinal cord injuries and more recently had entered into caring for people with brain injuries.

Along with each move came a news conference. Television and newspaper people would be asking questions about his long-term prognosis. Nobody really had any answers except that, because the brain is so complex, it would take several months of therapy before anyone could determine the extent of his disabilities.

We did know the most damaged part of his brain was the left frontal lobe. This area controls the right side of the body, hence there was little movement of the right arm and leg. His speech and short-term memory had also been affected. We came to believe damage on the surface of the brain might not be so permanent and Eddie might regain certain brain functions through therapy. The doctors couldn't report any more about Eddie's condition at that point. They did say he would have even harder work ahead of him than what he had already been through. The doctors seemed cautious about predicting the extent of his recovery.

For Thanksgiving, 11 weeks after his accident, Eddie had a taste of food. Seeing the sad expression on his face after tasting the mashed potatoes and gravy, I shuddered to think how long it would take for him to gain back the 75 pounds he had lost.

One afternoon I was making sales calls and listening to the radio when the sports news came on. The announcer reported Eddie Reinhardt had just spoken his first words. "Today, Eddie Reinhardt spoke his first words in four months. His mother was feeding him apple pie and he declared, 'I'm full!'" Immediately, I was on my way to the hospital as I rejoiced at another step forward. "If he can say two words, he can learn to say a thousand," I told myself.

Pat was surprised to see me in the middle of the day and unaware the news reached the media so quickly. While discussing his first words we remembered his voracious appetite before the injury. I commented the miracle was not that he spoke, but that he said the words, "I'm full."

When Eddie was in a coma and in bed, his physical limitations were not so obvious to me, but one day I visited the hospital at noon and found him in the physical therapy area lying on a mat. He was dressed in sweats and for a second resembled his old self. As I stood in the doorway watching the therapist coaxing him to lift his leg, I realized how limited my son really was. What he could have done without any effort before his injury, was now nearly impossible.

I couldn't bear to watch any more and hurried out of the hospital. I became aware of the young people wheeling around the hallways and in the hospital lobby. I walked faster and faster without running, all the time holding back the tears. The car seemed so far away. Finally, safely sitting in my car I was able to let go of my feelings about Eddie's tragedy. Again, I felt alone with no one to turn to.

I thought, "He survived a coma which had lasted two months, nearly died from pneumonia and now he is barely able to move his body." The reality of his injury continued to sink in. This was taking over my life, and as his father, I would be asked to give everything.

The Institutes for the Achievement of Human Potential

By mid-December we were bringing Eddie home for afternoon visits on Saturdays and Sundays, hoping to get acquainted with his care well enough to have him home overnight for Christmas. Preparations to move him to the car and into the house were complex. He had to be dressed for the weather and lifted into his wheelchair. Medicines had to be scheduled before and after meals and his mobile catheter bag had to be attached. Each step seemed difficult for us as we adjusted our schedules to care for him. During the five-mile trip home, we had to stop frequently for him to vomit because of motion sickness. Once at home he went right to bed, exhausted from the ride, and slept almost until it was time to go back to the hospital.

By Christmas Eve we felt confident enough to keep him overnight. Inch by inch we struggled to adjust to his needs. The kids talked to him constantly or read get well cards. His friends from college were coming home for Christmas and Eddie was able to acknowledge their remarks. His friends' reaction to his condition varied from shock and tears to their urging him, "Get off your butt and get well by my next visit." Eddie tried to console the hurting ones by reaching out and touching them.

One dad and his son sat in their car after their visit weeping. The two of them talked, and later I learned it was one of their closest times together as father and son.

By late January, the doctors thought Eddie had improved enough to be an outpatient; his discharge date was set for February 15, five months after his accident. My intensity continued at a high level as I frequently stopped by to watch his therapy. Swimming, speech, occupational and physical therapy took up most of his day. I found it difficult to function in other areas of my life when he was in such a wretched condition.

His appearance was frightful. His face was thin. His hair had been shaved on the left side with the middle measuring nearly an inch long and the right side measuring two or three inches. He couldn't sit in his wheelchair without a band around his waist tying him to the chair to prevent him from slipping out. He was unable to talk but could motion for things he wanted. He still had a catheter bag attached to his leg. His smile was crooked but still it helped make things tolerable for me. My anxiety for a faster recovery was nearly unbearable, especially after I realized how long it would take and how little I could do to speed up the process.

Once at home, our daily routine started early. Paul and Matt still were in elementary school. John was in college at Nebraska. Rosemarie left school at Wyoming for a semester to help out at home. Tom was a senior in high school. All of them had needs of their own, but I needed Tom's strength each morning to help me bring Eddie and his wheelchair up the stairs. I had rigged up a drive-in shower in the laundry room. It was temporary as we had construction underway on a 20 foot by 30 foot addition to our house which would include a roll-in shower; this was all possible from the contributions I tried to squelch.

The staff at Craig told us his outpatient program would finish in May, eight months after his accident and we wondered what would happen next. A parent of another brain-injured young man from Texas said they were told, "Take your kid home, make him comfortable and perhaps set up a three-or-four-hour-a-week-therapy program. Otherwise, that's about all you can do."

We were anxious about his upcoming release from the hospital. "Surely this isn't where life ends for Eddie," we thought. "There must be more we can do for him. We can't leave him in a wheelchair all his life, unable to speak or see clearly. Where can we go to learn more about how to help brain-injured people?" We began to search out answers to those questions.

After his injury and throughout the remainder of the 1984 football season, Eddie's condition was reported across the country. His survival so far had been considered a miracle, so we had lots of calls from the media asking about his progress. We always spoke with the hope he would continue getting better. However, we felt uncertain whether he would ever recover enough to function in society. It was difficult to remain hopeful as we watched his slow recovery. People called about their brain-injured children, telling us of the progress they had and the kinds of therapy they were using. We were told several times about a place in Philadelphia called The Institutes for the Achievement of Human Potential.

One phone call about The Institutes was from a couple in Arlington, Texas. I accepted their offer to visit them and learn what they were doing for their child hurt in a shooting accident. The father took early retirement to work with his wife to manage his son's recovery program. In April I spent two days at their home watching them do therapy in almost perpetual motion. From seven in the morning until eight at night, they did patterning and other kinds of therapy with more than a hundred volunteers a week. Patterning is a method of therapy where five people move the patients limbs and his head to simulate crawling. This goes on for five minutes. Following this, the disabled person is moved to the floor where he or she tries to crawl on his or her own, just like the brain had been conditioned to do during patterning. The procedure is repeated three times each hour, four times a day.

I was shocked to see their determination to help their 18-year-old son work to regain his mobility. He was shot through the front portion of his head. His intellectual functions were intact, but he remained motionless for two and a half years until the medical specialists told them to take him home because nothing more could be done for him. It was at that time they heard about The Institutes. After four years, they could watch their son creep on his hands and knees twice around their garage floor, a distance of 50 feet. I was optimistic to think we could be doing this for Eddie.

Pat and I went out for dinner the evening I got back from Texas to talk about all the information I had gathered. Pat wanted to hear every detail. Eventually, I said, "I don't know how we could ever do what they are doing, but I think we have to try." What Pat was hoping for was my commitment to this therapy program. She had read many books about The Institutes' program including, *What to Do About Your Brain Injured Child*, and was already drawn to this form of therapy. Though skeptical in the beginning, she began to see how important it was to offer structure and consistency to the brain injured person and the family. She could especially relate to the concept of frequency, intensity and duration in treating brain injury. The repetition needed to re-learn or recover what was lost seemed logical to her.

I had to figure out how I was going to continue working to support my family, continue raising the other children and do the therapy program, before I could make my commitment. I decided Eddie would have to come first.

The Institutes work primarily with the treatment of injured children, however, it has done extensive studies on the way healthy children learn and has written books titled, *How to Teach Your Child to Read, How to Teach Your Child Math*, and *How to Teach Your Child Another Language*. The principles of how healthy children learn is applied to those with brain injury. The Institutes have worked closely with NASA on solutions to balance and motion sickness. The prevalent belief at this facility is parents are determined to help their kids and will do the hard work required.

I was still grappling with how Eddie's accident and the circumstances of my relationship with my dad were strangely connected. Pat saw me struggle more and more with depression. She recognized my inability to perform just normal duties around home. Fortunately, I was self-employed, so I only had to interact with one employee and called on clients only on good days. She noticed I was withdrawn and lacked interest in anything except caring for Eddie.

Despite my new bond with my father, I still dwelt on my relationship with him and the pain I endured from his absence. Putting all my energy into Eddie's care, side-by-side with my wife did not fill the void in my heart. I needed to seek professional help.

After we had applied to The Institutes to admit Eddie for treatment, I began seeing a Christian counselor. He thought the synchronicity surrounding the events was a way for God to tell me I needed to change my life. My therapist walked me back through my early childhood, looking at my early relationship with my father. We recognized my behavior problems in school started after my father left home. We talked about the effect the lonely years had on me. I was always waiting for him to come home so we could live on a ranch together. The waiting stymied my growth in so many ways. I saw then, and can even see now, I was waiting for something to happen rather than making decisions.

According to the counselor, my specific behaviors—keeping my distance from others, not trusting God and resenting the help of others—were not unusual for a person deserted by his father.

"Deserted! I wasn't deserted!" I protested angrily. "My father never deserted me! He took a job during the war, and that job kept him in the Aleutian Islands for five years. He couldn't come home! After the war he just stayed on the West Coast and still didn't come home." I resented this counselor saying my father had deserted me and I decided I wasn't going back.

But I did go back because, down deep, I knew he was right. I had to admit Dad deserted me or I would not move beyond the deep-seated anger which was causing me so much trouble. I worked with him for three years. The counselor recognized my inability to articulate my feelings about Eddie's accident, my early years with Dad and my parents' divorce. He suggested I write down my feelings. Week after week I told him how frustrated I was about not being able to connect with my feelings long enough to write them down. He suggested I watch *I Never Sang For My Father*, an early 70s movie starring Gene Hackman and Melvyn Douglas, which garnered them Oscar nominations for their riveting performances. It's a sad movie about a father who withholds the unconditional love and approval the son seeks as he struggles to live up to his father's expectations and yet remain true to himself. He did everything for his father but never sang for him. He, too, couldn't get his life started until there was closure in their relationship. Unfortunately, the father dies without reconciling with his son.

The next weekend, Pat was in Nebraska visiting her parents and the kids were upstairs sleeping. It was about midnight when I decided to watch the movie. It helped me connect my feelings with my own father and I began to write. The day before, my counselor asked me to tell him how I felt when I was listening to the radio, the day I heard about Eddie's accident. I decided to start there. I remembered how crazy I was behaving on the drive home and how frightened I was about losing Eddie. It helped me identify what it meant to feel an emotion rather than to cover it up. So I began to write.

I moved on to the next question. "How did you feel at the time of your parents divorce?"

By now, my paper was dripping with tears. I could barely hold my pen to write. It was as if I were back in the courtroom. I felt the same emotions I did when I stood in front of the judge. Then, just 48 hours later, I had covered up those feelings with plans for my future and pretended the events hadn't really meant anything. As I wrote about this event, my guts ached and I was exhausted. I didn't finish until after 4:30 in the morning. I locked up 20 pages of my journal in a file cabinet before I went to bed. I decided neither I, nor anyone else would ever read my tear-stained attempt to say what I was really feeling about many of the sad parts of my life.

During the sessions which followed, I was asked similar questions—how did I feel about being asked to sign the papers to donate Eddie's organs, or the dream about Eddie playing basketball with Jesus and did I ever remove the fence separating myself from our Lord. Sometimes I was so anxious to write I would go to a motel alone, have dinner, keep the television off and begin to write. After two years and a few hundred pages, I was finished writing. I then locked the file cabinet where they would lay for the next 10 years.

At the same time I started therapy, Eddie began the long road which would take him from a wheelchair to running three miles in under 42 minutes. He would go from being patterned to crawling on his belly a thousand yards a day—with thick knee pads, creeping on his hands and knees, he would cover the distance of 40 football fields daily. He would progress from mumbling, "I'm full!" to singing country-western music.

While Eddie progressed, I developed in my own way. I began to let people be part of my life, and began to tear down the walls I had built. I continued to grow and I began working to make some good come from both of our struggles.

That's What Tough Is

*O*n the first anniversary of Eddie's accident, Saturday, September 14, 1985, the University of Colorado was scheduled to play the University of Oregon. This year, the game would be played in Boulder. The CU athletic department wanted to recognize the people of Oregon for all the help and support they gave our family during our month-long stay in Eugene. They decided to declare this "Ed Reinhardt Day."

A halftime program was planned to introduce dignitaries from the cities of Eugene and Boulder. This included the mayors of both cities and several people from the Eugene city council. In addition, Oregon's athletic director and members of his staff were recognized along with members of the medical staff from the Sacred Heart Hospital in Eugene, including Dr. Arthur Hockey.

A lot of planning was necessary in order for Eddie to participate in this event. Our home in Littleton is about 40 miles from Boulder and the trip would be tiring for him. Eddie still became nauseated riding in a car. Fatigue required us to have a place for him to rest. Medications would be carefully scheduled. A CU alumnus volunteered to have his motor home parked near the field-house so Eddie could nap before and after the game.

When we arrived at the stadium we were given a schedule of events for the afternoon with detailed instructions for our part of the halftime activities. Two naval cadets in dress whites would be our escorts.

At halftime, after the people from Eugene and Boulder had been recognized, Eddie was brought onto the field in a golf cart. The driver circled the field and stopped at the 50 yard line. I had insisted Eddie get out of the cart and stand between Pat and me. I assured the program director I would be by his side and he could lean on my shoulder as he stood and turned to wave to the crowd. I believed his fans needed to see his progress and having him stand seemed the best way to show it. Most of the media pictures taken previously showed him in a wheelchair.

With my assistance, Eddie was able to maneuver away from the cart and stand next to me and Pat. I whispered to him to turn and wave to the people around the stadium. He turned, making a complete circle, smiled and held his left arm high above his head. His 6 foot 7 inch frame and 37 inch arm reached out to the fans and seemed to touch each one of their hearts. The more he turned around to wave, the more deafening was the sound from the crowd as they chanted, "Ed-die, Ed-die."

The Colorado band stood on the field playing, "You'll Never Walk Alone," from Rodgers and Hammerstein's *"Carousel."* More than 40,000 fans cheered and waved back to Eddie. He stole their hearts that afternoon in Boulder as he stood straight and tall, waving and smiling.

Our oldest son John, who had finished playing football for the University of Nebraska, attended this game in Boulder. Afterward, he was interviewed by a TV reporter from Omaha, Nebraska, and had some thoughts about toughness:

Announcer: It has been an excited crowd today in Boulder for the homecoming of former Buffalo, Ed Reinhardt. Reinhardt, Number 88, was injured in a play in the Colorado-Oregon game last year and he nearly died of a blood clot. He spent two months in a coma, and it seems a miracle he lives today. This is Ed's first trip back to Folsom Field since the accident in Oregon and his brother John who played middle guard for Nebraska last year is here.

John: For me, it was one of the greatest days of my life, to see him come through when he was so close to death. And for him, today was a big payoff.

Announcer: A payoff for a year of hard work which far exceeds any of the effort he put forth to play college football.

John: The work Ed has to do is seven days a week, 24 hours a day. Every day when he gets up in the morning, it's a fight to go through his daily life. His injury is a continual thing he has to fight and get better from.

Announcer: He has shown tremendous improvement by his return to Folsom Field. His battle has affected numerous people including his brother John whose perspective on many things has changed. Football is no longer a measure for toughness.

John: You know, you read the stories where some coaches will actually have their players perform some violent ritual like stomp on frogs to get them excited. It's not tough to do that; it's tough if you're injured and come back—that's what tough is.

John's remarks have strengthened me more than anything else I have heard or read throughout Eddie's rehabilitation. As the years of work with Eddie continued, those words and my promise to Eddie made me tougher in my fight to bring him back.

After the game, during a social function for the dignitaries from Oregon, Pat and I had a chance to visit with some of them and with members of the medical team who had cared for Eddie. Even George Lamont from the chicken farm was there.

I also had the opportunity to meet the Oregon alumni member, an attorney from Eugene, who paid to have Pat, Rosemarie, and John, flown from Lincoln, to Eugene the night of Eddie's accident in a chartered jet at the cost of $9,500. I wanted to thank him personally for his generosity to my family.

Before we ended our conversation, I asked him if he had known another attorney named Frank Reid, who practiced law in Eugene during the early '50s. "Yes, I knew Frank Reid; he was a good lawyer and a good friend of mine. He later became a district court judge in Eugene. Frank passed away a few years ago. Did you know him?"

I hesitated. I lost my breath for a moment and felt stunned by the same fear I had standing outside the courtroom the day of my parents' divorce. Finally I said, "Yes, years ago, my family needed an attorney for a legal matter in Eugene and a relative suggested Mr. Reid. It was thirty-two years ago. I was just a kid. I don't remember much about him except he was a good man."

I remembered Mr. Reid very well. In fact, I can still picture him leaning close to my face and whispering directions to me about the things that were going to happen in that courtroom. I am also reminded of the sound of the gavel that still rings in my ears and the judge's announcement, "Divorce granted."

Where Miracles Happen

One month after Ed Reinhardt Day we were walking the halls at The Institutes for the Achievement of Human Potential located off Stenton Avenue in Northwest Philadelphia. As we drove into the walled, gated area, we could see an old mansion almost completely closed in with trees and bushes. We parked back behind the main building, which had been donated to a small group of medical doctors and therapists back in the 1950s.

Several buildings are used as clinics where they do patient evaluations and where they design therapy programs for patients who will go home and work before returning six months later. Farther down the steep drive are residential buildings where patients come to stay so they can be studied daily as research participants.

The reception area still displays the portrait of the donor's wife hanging on the wall. After signing in, we moved to a gathering room where 28 other couples and their brain-injured children were waiting for their call to begin evaluations.

"Oh, God! What is this? How did I get into this mess?" I thought, as I looked around and saw children everywhere laying and crawling on the floor which was covered with gymnastic mats. Some were crying and making strange sounds. There were no chairs, just benches around the wall. I learned later the floor could be a treatment method for the child. Lying prone on the

170

floor encouraged the child to strengthen his arms, to lift his chest and eventually to begin crawling. Parents were laying on the floor with their children trying to comfort them while awaiting evaluation.

I felt completely out of place and wanted to leave. Eddie at 19 was much older than all the other kids. His age and size made me feel we didn't belong. "God-damn! How will our lives ever get back to normal?" I fought myself all that day, telling myself we were not like the others. I kept thinking I had other things I should be doing. I glanced around again at the faithful parents lying on the floor and began to accept maybe I was in the best place for Eddie.

The week-long schedule began with two initial days of extensive evaluations in visual, auditory, and tactile competence, along with evaluation of mobility, language and manual abilities.

Pat and I spent the next three days and evenings in class learning about brain function and how their method of therapy could help Eddie. They wanted to know as much about me and Pat as they did about him. We were all being evaluated.

Glen Doman, the director and one of the founders of The Institutes, stated, "This is an unreasonable therapy program for an unreasonable problem." His discourse, on one hand, seemed to discourage us from taking on this work which would demand so much from all of us. Then in the same breath, he reminded us perhaps no other therapy could be as effective as their program. Mr. Doman claimed to have more data on brain therapy than any place else in the world.

During the general sessions with all the parents, Mr. Doman shared his story about how some people in the medical community shunned The Institutes. He told about a couple who was visiting the umpteenth doctor with their brain injured child. The doctor said to them, "Don't do something foolish like taking your child to that place in Philadelphia." The child's father went immediately out in the hall to call for information about The Institutes in Philadelphia.

Mr. Doman has given so much of his life to helping people in an area where there is so little research and so few answers. He exudes unselfishness and love for the young people struggling with brain dysfunction caused by injury or from lack of oxygen. He says many times during his lectures, "The Institutes is the place parents bring their children after they have tried everything else."

During our early visits to The Institutes, Mr. Doman would reminisce about his life experiences and about his time in the army during World War II. He was a company commander assigned to an infantry outfit in Patton's army. He started out fighting in Africa, moved through Italy and was nearing Berlin when the war ended. He told about the many battles, the casualties and of men dying in his arms. "As an infantry company commander of 187 men and 6 officers, we were three times reduced to 18 men and no officers. In all the world there is no greater pacifist than a victorious combat infantry soldier at the end of a war—unless it is possibly a defeated combat infantry soldier. I spent four and a half years blowing the brains out of young men and a lifetime helping people put brains back together."

I trusted Glen Doman. I wanted to believe him. From him, I got another glimpse of what it must be like to have a real father. Hope is what he gave me—the hope Eddie could get better. That hope was all I needed; we would do the work.

After a week of early meetings and late night classes, we found ourselves frightened and exhausted. We had learned just enough during the week to think we might not be accepted. We were just short of planning to beg them to accept us for Eddie's sake when we were called into the library of the mansion which adjoined the clinic.

It was after midnight when we were directed into the dimly lit, dark-wood-finished, conference room where we sat with three therapists and Mr. Doman, waiting for their verdict. Mr. Doman began by reviewing Eddie's evaluation chart. "Eddie is profoundly brain injured," he said. "Some functions may be improved by therapy, if— that's a big if—IF you follow the program we have set up for you. It is intense and demanding. It will take all you've got. Your lives will never be the same. If you decide to do this program, you will become so well organized, other people will seem to be moving in slow motion.

"There are no holidays or days off. You will work from morning until night and you will need all the volunteers you can find." He then hesitated and looked at the three of us for a long time. "You have been accepted into the clinic. Go home and think it over. When you've made your decision, call us back and tell us you are ready to begin Eddie's therapy program. The success of his program is in your hands."

By Wednesday of the following week we called back and told Mr. Doman we were ready to begin the work. We placed notices in schools and church bulletins and asked around the neighborhood for volunteers. We would need 140 people each week as well as a substitute list. Each crew had five people: one on each of Ed's limbs, one to move his head. The volunteers came at 6:30 A.M., 9:30 A.M., 3:30 P.M. and 7:00 P.M.

Some of what they did was called patterning. Patterning is the most well known and the most misunderstood of the many therapy techniques offered by the Institutes. In the case of a small child, three adults carry a child's body through the movements of crawling. Because of Eddie's size we would need five volunteers. One adult would turn Ed's head while others would move the arms and legs while Ed lay prone on a treatment table.

The patterning is not to strengthen arms and legs but to give a message to the brain. The message says, "This is how it feels to crawl, this is how it feels to move." There would be many techniques to stimulate the brain. Our marching orders were to use frequency, intensity and duration. We always had a clip board and a stop watch. All this fit right into his athletic background.

After the long days of therapy, Pat went to her little office in the basement to prepare the next day's reading material. The material was supposed to be college level to keep challenging Eddie. She made large print books containing biographies of Desmond Tutu, Winston Churchill, Robert Frost and John Elway.

As reported in the November 14, 1994, Sports Illustrated, former Colorado football Coach Bill McCartney, shakes his head in wonder. "The real story is this family unit," he says. "This is all about faith, and their faith never wavers. There is no limit to what they will do. They don't look around and say, 'where is the help coming from,' they just press on. Such love. When this accident happened, they didn't even break stride. There is just something inside the Reinhardt family. They have this drive and intensity. And that woman.

"She is blue twisted steel." Pat was always uncomfortable with being blue twisted steel. She told me, "It doesn't sound very cuddly." I replied, "Well, cuddly isn't everything."

Three weeks later, Eddie was working 12 hours a day, seven days a week. The first group of five volunteers would arrive at 6:20 each morning. In case a helper didn't show up at the last minute, we would pull either Matt, Tom or Paul out of bed to help. I monitored the first crew and filled in if necessary. After that, Pat would take over and I'd go to work. I would work with the evening volunteers and the weekend crews.

The volunteers kept coming. They were always kind and cheerful with Ed and their positive comments were helpful for us. Because they weren't immersed in the therapy each day like we were, they could see changes we couldn't. Hearing about what they saw helped me persevere.

In another six months we were back at The Institutes. By now, Eddie was able to sit through some of the training lectures. His concentration had improved enough for them to intensify his intellectual therapy. Also, his dose of anti-seizure medicine was being reduced in tiny increments each month. This helped him become more alert.

In January of 1987, nearly three years after the accident, we were offered time off from the program. They said we wouldn't have to re-start the program again until we were ready to work for another two years. We persevered through the spring of 1987, and by the Fourth of July, we were on vacation.

During our time away from therapy, I decided it was time to go back to Oregon. I wanted to fulfill a promise I had made to the people who worked at the hospital the day we flew out of Oregon. I promised someday we would come back when Ed was able to walk into their hospital and talk to those who were so much a part of his recovery.

The walk through Sacred Heart Hospital on that Friday afternoon in October 1987, and meeting the medical personnel and friends in Eugene, helped me with my healing process. We toured the intensive care unit and stepped into what had been Eddie's room. As I peered out the window, I saw the familiar red neon sign which spelled out "EUGENE HOTEL" still shining down the street. The staff had arranged a reception for us, and as they arrived, Eddie sang the Kenny Rogers' song, "The Gambler" and "Thank God for Kids" by Eddy Raven. During this reception, he first sang in public. He did so well someone suggested he might have a career in music. He looked so well, before the party was over, one of the nurses was sitting on his lap.

I didn't want to leave Eugene until I had returned to the football field and had walked out to the 37 yard line where he had been injured. I believed this would provide closure for me.

Upon returning to Colorado, my counseling moved forward. Week after week I saw the counselor and we talked, always working to understand the circumstances between my two tragic events in Oregon. Eventually, I learned it was less important they happened in the same city. What was important, he said, was what I did with my life because of them. We talked at length about Romans 8:28: "All things happen for good to those who love God and who are called according to his purpose." I finally understood it was up to me to begin to fit into His plan in order to make something good come from such a tragedy.

"You're OK, Kid!"

CHAPTER 28

During January of 1990, six years after Eddie's accident, I began hearing that same little voice I recognized as the Spirit of God coaxing me to go back to visit my dad one more time. It seemed the more I tried to still this voice, the more insistent it became. So, in early March I made arrangements to go see Dad. From the beginning I believed this meeting would be our last time together, and I wanted it to be a time when I could once again experience what it was like to be my father's son. I hoped somehow, through that experience, I could learn what it was like to be a son of God.

Many times throughout my young life I was unable to know and understand what a father-son relationship was all about. Therefore any relationship I had with God was incomplete, which confused and frustrated me. I desperately needed to feel like a son—even at my age—if only for a few days. I wanted to go to bed at night in Dad's home, knowing he was sleeping down the hall. I wanted to know how it felt to wake up in the morning and know my dad was in the kitchen.

I was weary of always "being my own father." It seemed as if I had been the father for so long and for so many people, I could barely remember being just a little boy with my own father. Growing up in a fatherless home, I had lots of work and responsibilities placed on my shoulders. Later, as the father of six

176

children, there was seldom any relief or a place or time to lay down my burden and rest.

Realizing this visit could be my last experience as a son, I also wanted Dad to experience his position as a father so he could feel loved by a son without having any guilt for his neglect of me. I desperately needed to show him, even if I couldn't tell him, he was forgiven for deserting me.

I guess I really wanted to feel my life was in order. I felt all I needed to feel secure was to know I was loved by my dad. I believe order in a normal family requires a caring father and a loving mother. It is the responsibility of parents to pass down their love to the next generation. It is terribly difficult to give our children something we didn't receive when we were young. I had to visit my dad again before it was too late.

All of my dreams about being with Dad were fulfilled during those four days. It was better than I ever imagined. Even though I was 57 years old and he was 89, I hung on to his every word as he talked about the Oregon weather, the mountains, building roads in Alaska, his ranch in Grants Pass, and his life as a cowboy from Wyoming to Texas. I especially liked listening to the few memories he had about his own father. For the first time, I felt proud of being named after my father and grandfather and decided when I got back home, I would change my name back to Floyd.

Perhaps he didn't make much out of the family part of his life because he hadn't had any relationship skills or tools given to him as a child. As his son, I could accept the effort he did make. By all standards, he was successful in his work life. I respected him for the effort he had put forth to make something of himself. I will always be thankful he gave me life.

As the time for me to leave him and go back to Denver drew near, I sensed within me the same feelings I'd had as a little boy saying goodbye to him. I remembered that Saturday morning when I was nine, when he first left home for Wyoming and the lonely years that followed. After the divorce, when we said goodbye again, the sadness followed me for so many years.

This time our goodbye would be different. I knew, because of this visit, I would leave him knowing what love really meant between a father and a son. Finally I could leave having a better understanding of what it was like to be loved by a father.

I said goodbye to my brothers and sister and their families and moved closer to the door where Dad was standing. I leaned over and gave him a hug and whispered quietly, "I love you Dad; I've always loved you." As I loosened my arms from around his shoulders, he looked up at me, and, with a firm but gentle voice said, "You're OK, Kid!" With my voice cracking and with tears streaming down my face, I said, "Thanks, Dad." I turned and walked away.

The flight home was like the many Sunday night trips I had made throughout my business career. I was alone and was thankful I had some time to lean back in the seat and think about my time with Dad, how slight and fragile he seemed. He hardly weighed 140 pounds now. Dad had always liked the stories of the brave men of the West and lived the wandering life style of a cowboy. His favorite old timer was Buffalo Bill Cody. William Cody was also from Nebraska and at one time had a large cattle ranch near North Platte. Dad attended many of the Buffalo Bill Wild West shows in Omaha. His admiration for Buffalo Bill encouraged him to trim his facial hair like Cody's with a wide mustache and a narrow beard down from his chin.

As I reminisced, it just felt good to love him for all of those reasons. None of his past wrongs mattered much anymore. I was at peace with my feelings toward Dad after our time together. I felt a reverence for him I felt for few other people in my life. "Why shouldn't I? He is my Dad." Finally, I could claim having a dad to love and respect, without reservation.

Pat was still awake when I got home. Pat always liked to hear about an event from start to finish. Just telling her "It was a great trip" was never sufficient, so I repeated the stories Dad told about his youth and the events of his life in the West and on his ranch in Oregon. Pat had heard most of them before during other visits and was anxious to hear more about what happened between Dad and me. She recognized my former resentment of him had finally given way when I mentioned all the good times we had during our visit. Pat and I laughed when I tried to explain his mustache and how much he really did look like Buffalo Bill Cody. She turned her nose a little when I told her he still chewed tobacco.

Then, my emotions changed when I considered telling her what he had told me as I was leaving to come home. Pat sensed my tale was incomplete.

"What else did he say?"

"Oh, not much. He just said I was OK." I said it in a small, quiet voice as I pretended to look into the closet for something. Pat walked up behind me and asked me to tell her what else my Dad had said to me, as though she had been there and knew what he said.

As I turned, she could see the tears flowing down my face. I held her in my arms and I began to sob when I tried to say something more to her. She realized I wasn't able to go on, and her arms tightened around my neck. We held each other until I caught my breath and mumbled a few words about saying goodbye to Dad. "Well, he just said, 'You're OK, Kid'. I told him I loved him and that's when he said it. He just said, 'You're OK Kid!' I thought about it all the way home. I keep saying it over and over. As I was leaving, I just told him I loved him, and that's what he said."

Pat said, "I'm happy you had that time together with your dad. I know he loves you, Ed. He's told me before how much he admires you. He knows you better than you know yourself. He sees things in you that you don't even realize. That's what he was telling you. That's his way of telling you he loves you. You don't realize how much you mean to him. I think you're his favorite son."

A few months later, Dad's life on earth ended. We buried him next to my mother in Omaha, and although they had been separated for 42 years in life, I was comforted I had brought them together again.

Now, every day I listen and I hear his same soft voice telling me, "You're OK, Kid!"

Discovering Our Ministries

*T*he Institutes suggested Eddie take voice lessons to help his speech, so they were added to his already overloaded weekly schedule. After two years of lessons, his music therapy began to show results. His speech also improved as he developed his talent to sing country-western music. We learned control for speaking is located in the front left part of the brain, while music comes from a different area. His singing teacher told us there was no damage in the musical part of his brain and he had excellent timing and near perfect pitch. I thought this new talent could enhance his outgoing personality and maybe a career could be developed through music.

Word got around about his singing and he was asked to sing during a University of Colorado awards banquet. Andy Bryant, an alumni member and a good family friend, called from Boulder to ask me if Eddie could sing at Coach Bill McCartney's Friday morning men's prayer meeting. Eddie agreed to sing for them.

During the week that followed Andy's phone call, I couldn't stop thinking about how much I needed to share my experience with other men about my relationship with my dad. Maybe I could trust my feelings with this group of Christian men. I called Andy back and told him about the recent death of my dad and his funeral in Omaha a few weeks before. I also said to him I was trying to understand why Eddie's accident had happened in Eugene, where I faced so many other issues long before Eddie's accident. I told him how baffled I was about the two events and how sharing my story with some Christian men whom I could trust, might help me sort it all out.

Andy called back after making some changes in their meeting program and said I could talk to the men the following week and Eddie could come up the week after me.

"I could never do this," I thought, after hanging up the phone. "Why did I agree to do this? I can't get up in front of a hundred men and tell my story. I have to call him back and postpone the date. God, why do I get into these deals?" Public speaking had always been difficult for me. I had always felt a lack of confidence in believing I knew what I was talking about. "This occasion is different," I thought. "I can talk about myself and share my story."

No outsiders knew the story of what really happened surrounding Eddie's accident. There certainly had been some strange coincidences, and this group of men might like to hear about my relationship with my own father and how it strangely connects with Eddie's accident." My confidence began to grow until I even felt excited about the event.

Eddie was walking two to three miles a day for his therapy. Every afternoon after work, I took him over to Heritage High School to walk around the football field. Day after day I walked with him and practiced my talk. Eddie got tired of listening to me talk about Dad, so he decided to walk in the other direction. Occasionally, he turned his head away from me when we passed, or reached out with his tremendous left arm to take a playful swing at me. Eddie had always been suspicious about my dad after learning how he had treated his family. I had to explain to him how we have to forgive others. Eddie wasn't so sure he could but, more often than not, he ended our conversations by saying, "Grandpa, pretty good guy!"

Andy Bryant had a friend in Boulder who owned one of the finest hotels in town. He arranged for me to come to Boulder the night before I was to share my story and stay at the hotel to save me the early morning drive from my home in Littleton.

I was scared during the drive up, scared before going to bed and I woke up scared. My notes were in order and I knew all I had to do was follow my notes. How could I tell a group of men I had told my dad I loved him? Guys don't tell other men things like that!

I kept asking myself, "Why did I want to share my story so badly before, and now I don't want to do it at all? What if my voice isn't prepared for this, and what if I begin to cry, telling them about my parents' divorce. Oh, God! Why did I do this? Coach McCartney might be there, and then what? Why did I ask Andy if I could share my story? There is no way out now, I have to go through with it." I woke up early and I couldn't go back to sleep.

Coach McCartney was there that morning, which didn't make it any easier for me. I asked him to autograph my copy of his book, *Ashes to Glory* a book about his new men's organization called Promise Keepers. The book included a chapter entitled "Ed Reinhardt: Profile of a Winner."

I have read the chapter frequently and appreciate Coach McCartney's remarks about Eddie: "Years from now, when the history of the University of Colorado football program is written, it may be said of Ed Reinhardt that he made more of a significant contribution than any other human being." I tried to convince myself this comment was the reason I was there that morning. I also tried to remind myself of my newly found Scripture in Romans 8:28; "All things happen for good to those who love God and who are called according to his purpose."

I repeated this passage over and over before being introduced to speak. Finally, I told myself something good must come from Eddie's accident and by sharing our story this morning, something positive could happen. I thought it was my job to make that good happen.

I made a few light-hearted remarks about injecting myself into Eddie's invitation to sing, and then became serious about my need to share my experience with them about my own dad. Most of the men were older than I, and I learned later many of them still had unsettled business with their own fathers or sons.

I shared my story, pausing to regain control of my emotions several times when it became difficult to speak. I still could not admit to them my dad had deserted me. Thinking back, I wished I had. You could hear a pin drop when I told them about walking up to Dad's door after 20 years and introducing myself. I saw some men were crying when I repeated Dad's final words, "You're OK, Kid!"

I closed my testimony by declaring how much it meant to me to hear those words from my father. The same words coming from anyone else wouldn't have made the same impact on me as they had made coming from him. I explained how much we fathers influence the lives of our children and how there is hardly any escape or change from what our children learn from us. At the end I challenged them to reach out to their own fathers or sons if they had unfinished business.

Several men stayed after the meeting to share their experiences about their own fathers. One man said, with tears streaming down his face, "You talk about a relationship. My dad chased me out of the house with a shotgun, let me run for twenty yards and then fired. I didn't look back and I never saw my dad again."

Another fellow told me he was the son of a minister and explained how the only attention he got from his dad was after he had memorized a new scripture. He told me how much he began to resent the Bible and how he stayed away from church for over 20 years before finding the Lord in his own way.

I stayed around until all the men had left the hall and finally had a chance to talk with Coach McCartney. He always wanted to know what Eddie was doing and about the progress he was making. He thanked me for sharing my story and made a comment which would impact my future, "Men need to hear this story."

His words kept going through my head during the next several weeks. After telling Gretchen, one of Eddie's volunteers about our program, She suggested I contact the leader of the men's ministry at her church and share our story during their Saturday morning service. I still was not aware of the power my experience had until I listened to them tell their own stories after my talk. They encouraged me to continue sharing my experience with other men.

During the next few years, I accepted invitations to speak three or four times a year. I spoke about the strong influence fathers have in the lives of their children and challenged listeners to repair broken family relationships.

Eddie's musical abilities continued to develop and soon he began to share the stage with me. "Why not team up," I thought. "People certainly know him and know of his miracle recovery from the football accident. His music is entertaining, and he's an inspiration to anyone going through trouble." From then on, we would be introduced as Ed and Eddie Reinhardt, and our program is called, "You're OK, Kid!" As a fellow said introducing us recently, "Two Eds are better than one." Eddie starts our program with an enthusiastic delivery of his memorized speech.

"Several years ago I had a tragedy. I was a football star for the University of Colorado. I was the second leading pass receiver in the nation. My grade point average was 3.6. In the second game of my sophomore year, I caught a pass and was tackled. My head hit the ground very hard. I was in a coma for 62 days. The injury was a subdural-hematoma complicated by pneumonia. Doctors said it was a miracle I survived. Some people were sure I was destined to stay in a vegetative state. I threw myself into rehabilitation with the same work ethic I had as a football player. It took five months before I could speak. It took two years to learn to walk. My intelligence is intact and I am a great listener. Because of neurological damage, I find it difficult to put my thoughts into words. This talk I am giving now had to be memorized word for word. If we have a conversation, I would understand what you were saying, but I won't be able to tell you everything I want to say. (pause) I am disappointed I've lost the use of some of my body…and some of my mind. But, standing up here, looking into your wonderful eyes…LIFE IS WORTHWHILE."

I began reading everything I could about fatherhood and memorized statistics for my presentations. My reading included books like *Fatherless America* by David Blankenhorn, founder and president of the Institute for American Values. He could hardly finish page one in his introduction before saying, "Fatherlessness is the most harmful demographic trend of this generation. It is the leading cause of declining child well-being in our society. It is also the engine driving our most urgent social problems, from crime to adolescent pregnancy, to child sexual abuse to domestic violence against women. Yet, despite its scale of social consequences, fatherlessness is a problem frequently ignored or denied." Former vice-president Dan Quayle's comments about *Murphy Brown* have been vindicated. In 1992, he said, "It doesn't help matters when prime time TV has Murphy Brown—a character who supposedly epitomizes today's intelligent, highly paid, professional women—mocking the importance of fathers, by bearing a child alone and calling it just another lifestyle choice."

"In fact we seem to go out of our way to avoid the connection between our most pressing social problems and the trend of fatherlessness," Mr. Blankenhorn says in closing his introduction. "A good society celebrates the ideal of the man who puts his family first."

Judith S. Wallerstein is considered to be the world's foremost authority on the effects of divorce on children Her book, *The Unexpected Legacy of Divorce*, based on a 25-year landmark study, determined " children from divorced and remarried families are more aggressive toward their parents and teachers. They experience more depression, have more learning difficulties and suffer from more problems with peers than children from intact families. Children from divorced and remarried families are two to three times more likely to be referred for psychological help at school than their peers from intact families. More of them end up in mental health clinics and hospital settings. There is earlier sexual activity, more children born out of wedlock, less marriage and more divorce." In her research, Ms. Wallerstein learned that divorce is a life-transforming experience. After divorce, childhood is different. Adolescence is different. Adult-hood—with the decision to marry or not and have children or not—is different. Whether the final outcome is good or bad, the whole trajectory of an individual's life is profoundly altered by the divorce experience.

Dr. James Dobson says in his latest book, *Bringing Up Boys,* "It might be too late for society to bring our young men back from the secular world. If we do, it will be done by fathers." Dr. Dobson is a licensed psychologist with a Ph.D. in Child Development, and founder/president of Focus on the Family.

I ask myself, "If fathers caused most of the problems in our society by deserting and neglecting their children, how do we expect them to turn around and change the direction in which their children are going. I believe we need a wake up call!"

Coach McCartney, at his men's meetings around the country, frequently tells about a prison chaplain who decided to provide Mother's Day cards for prisoners to send to their mothers. The program was so successful, he had to go out and get more cards. He decided to do the same program for Father's Day, but none of the cards left the prison. Not one!

Coach McCartney, in his role as founder of Promise Keepers, declares over half of our children will go to bed tonight without a father in the home. He reports, without a father a child is more likely to:

1. Trail peers in moral development
2. Make bad choices in career decisions
3. Display a negative spirit instead of a positive outlook
4. Be robbed of a deep sense of personal security
5. Experience difficulty in sex role identification

McCartney added, "Fatherlessness is our biggest problem threatening the stability of America, causing our long-term national security to be at stake."

Passing On a Spiritual Legacy

*O*ur connection with Eugene is still not over. Every day I find an occasion where I am reminded of that part of my life: An Oregon license plate or a person I meet who lived in or attended school in Eugene. I've met many people who actually attended the game. I even met the referee who took the ball from Eddie after the tackle who explained how Eddie got up and trotted off the field just before he collapsed at the bench.

In 1997, I had a decision to make about going to Eugene to present our program to several local civic organizations. While driving around Denver thinking about my decision I noticed cars both in front and behind me with Oregon plates. My decision was made.

Ten years after Eddie was injured, our youngest son Matthew, who was a big tight end like Eddie, was graduating from Heritage High School in Littleton. He was now being recruited by many of the West Coast teams, including Oregon. Like John, Eddie and Tom, Matthew took his five trips to visit the colleges he might consider attending. Coach Rich Brooks, the same head coach of Oregon who recruited Eddie, called and asked us if he could contact Matthew. It seemed ironic to me Matthew might play for the university involved with Eddie's accident.

When he returned from his recruiting visit to Eugene, Matthew didn't hesitate to report he had decided to play for the

University of Oregon. Matthew was red-shirted (placed on reserve) during his freshman year, giving him a year to adjust to college life and grow stronger in order to be able to play football at the college level as a sophomore. We attended many games in Eugene. I had good times uniting with some of our friends again to show them how well Eddie was doing. George Lamont, the flying chicken farmer, gave Eddie and me a ride in his latest airplane.

I felt at peace being back in Eugene. The neon sign "EUGENE HOTEL" still faithfully lit up the night sky. My attitude had changed a lot since my last visit. I had so much faith good things were happening because of Eddie's accident. Just being in Eugene again was joyful for me. We had dinner in the restaurant, formerly the little ice cream store on the corner of Broadway and Pearl, with Pat's aunt and uncle, Art and Helen Richter. They came down from Seattle for the first game of the season to see Matt play.

Pat reminded me of a conversation she had with Matthew before he started his freshman year. While they were shopping for school clothes, Matthew remarked, "Wouldn't it be great if Oregon won the Pac-Ten League and I could play in the Rose Bowl." Pat smiled at his naivete. Oregon hadn't played in the Rose Bowl in over 40 years. Well, Oregon did win enough games to qualify to play in the Rose Bowl and we were ecstatic about going to another bowl game.

It didn't take the Reinhardts long to get packed up for that game. We attended the Rose Bowl Parade in Pasadena and arrived at the stadium early to watch Matthew's pre-game practice. During the game, he was in a dozen or so times, mostly on special teams plays like kick-offs and punt returns. Unfortunately, Joe Paterno's Penn State Nittany Lions were victorious.

During the following summer, Matt's brothers noticed he was not working out at the recreation center as much as they thought he should. He wasn't running each evening as they had all done before to fill the requirements of their summer conditioning programs. At Nebraska, John had to fill out a card reporting the results of his conditioning each weekend and then be tested on those reports the first day of practice. I noticed Matthew was spending more time in his room after work and less time with his friends. He seemed to be preoccupied with something more important than preparing himself to play football. He asked to go to a religious retreat in Connecticut called "Test Your Call." We made arrangements for him to attend. After the retreat he returned excited about his experience.

By mid-August, Matthew was back in Eugene. Two days later, he called home and said, "Dad, I don't belong here anymore. I've been thinking about my future for a long time, especially this summer, and I believe I'm being called to serve the Lord. It wouldn't be good for me or the football team if I stayed here any longer. I want to leave school. I bought a one-way ticket with the money I earned this summer and I'm going to Connecticut to enter the seminary. I have a two-hour layover in Denver in the morning. I'll see you then."

Pat and I were shocked, "Wow! Where did this idea come from?" It didn't take me long to figure it out. As I looked back over Matt's life I could see he was being prepared to work in ministry for the Lord. I remembered the time he insisted he and I answer an altar call during a Billy Graham crusade at Mile High Stadium in Denver. At other times the question was posed, "Have you ever thought of giving your life to do God's work?" And Matthew went forward. Now, his mother and I were proud and overjoyed with his decision.

Matthew has now finished his studies in Mexico City and is currently stationed in Atlanta, where he works as a spiritual director and guidance counselor at a high school of the Legionaires of Christ. Through Matthew's calling to serve the Lord, I continue finding good which comes from tragedy. I have asked myself many times since Matthew left Oregon, "If my family had dissolved before Eddie's accident, would Matthew have heard this call? Would he have heard any calling for that matter, or would he have built walls around himself and others to protect himself from getting hurt? Would a divorce and my unkept promises as a father cause him a lifetime of sadness and disappointment? Would he have missed out on the greatest calling I believe a person can have, of giving his life to Christ and His mission here on earth?"

THE END

Brain Injury—
The Silent Epidemic

"*T*oday, Americans with traumatic brain injury are among the most underserved and the most neglected people in our population. Traumatic Brain Injury (TBI) is in fact, the leading killer and disabler of this country's children and young adults."

According to Allan I. Bergman, president and CEO of the National Brain Injury Association, over 5.3 million children and adults who were hospitalized with TBI are alive today. Recently, more seniors are suffering from TBI caused from falls. Medical costs for brain injury are astronomical! Lack of medical insurance is a huge problem. In 1994, the number of uninsured increased to 44 million people or 16 percent of the population and by 2007, it is predicted 25 percent, or 75 million people will not have medical insurance. More people are surviving and being cared for by relatives than ever before. They usually live at home with parents and often with only the mother. Mr. Bergman also reported 80 percent of families dissolve after experiencing a tragic accidental death or a life-changing injury to a family member.

Since Eddie's injury in 1984, I have become intimately acquainted with this "silent epidemic" and have learned how little is done for brain injury research and therapy. Learning about The Institute for the Achievement of Human Potential in Philadelphia, The Center for Cure of Paralysis at Jackson Memorial

Hospital in Miami and the Melvin Smith Learning Center in California did not come through any national directory or advice from a medical facility here in Denver. Eddie received enough national exposure that people called from all over the country to tell us about such services. Most are not so fortunate to get those calls.

For several years, Pat and I responded to calls from friends asking us to visit parents of children with brain injuries. Like us, they had no conception of the outcome of the injury, where to go to get an evaluation, and no idea what therapy could be done to help their children.

I struggled to do something to change this national crisis. I started by closing our "You're OK, Kid!" programs with a reminder that brain injury is known as the "silent epidemic." People were shocked to learn more than 2 million people are substantially brain-injured each year in the United States, 3,500 of them right in my home state of Colorado. The more I shared with my audience about brain injury, the more I realized there is no specific spokesperson for promoting research for this disability. We hear plenty about the heart association, breast cancer, and AIDS, and we watch and listen to Christopher Reeve raise millions for spinal cord injury.

But who is speaking for brain injury?

During the fall of 1999, I became concerned enough to make an appointment with Eddie's neurosurgeon, Dr. Glenn Kindt at the University of Colorado Health Sciences Center. I had just listened to Ms. Denise Brown, chief planning officer for the University of Colorado Health Sciences Center speak at a Lions Club in downtown Denver.

Ms. Brown thanked the Lions for their large donation for the eye research institute to be built next door to the new CU Health Sciences Center. "Why not build a National Research Center for Brain Injury at the same location?" I thought. I believed Colorado would be a natural place for such a project. It would be centrally located in the United States and the quality of medical personnel are some of the best in the country. Besides all of this, the weather is great.

My hands were wet and I was shaking when I sat down with Dr. Kindt. After sharing our experience of bringing Eddie home from Oregon 15 years earlier in the medical plane, I began telling him about the great need people have for a centralized medical facility for brain research.

Halfway through my description of what I thought was needed, I noticed I began talking faster and louder. I could feel he was about to interrupt me to tell me thanks for my interest, but such a facility wasn't needed and would be impossible to build at the new site. Instead, he waited until I finished and excitedly said, "I can't believe you're telling me this! This is a project we've been talking about for months." He wanted me to talk to his staff about my ideas.

The staff members were curious about my interest in brain injury and invited me to share my ideas in their monthly staff meeting. Our short talk emphasized the frustration that families feel in searching for help for brain injury. I talked about the need for a national research center for brain injury. This gave me the opportunity to suggest that the University of Colorado Health Sciences Center would be the ideal location for such a facility.

Maybe even more than my words, Eddie's stage presence and singing, garnered votes for my dream. The enthusiastic listeners clapped in time with the music when he sang the John Denver classic, "Thank God I'm a Country Boy."

I have learned building a brain injury facility like this takes years to complete. In the meantime I'll continue praying someday a national research center will become a reality in Denver.